Ignite

Pushing yourself outside of your comfort zone

AF506984

Jennifer Logan

Copyright © 2024

All Rights Reserved

ISBN: 979-8-89409-559-2

Dedication

To my dearest family,

This book is dedicated to the ones who mean the world to me – my immediate family.

Firstly, to my loving husband, Etienne Fox Logan II, thank you for loving me endlessly. I feel incredibly blessed to have your unwavering support in all my career endeavors. You are not just an amazing man but a wonderful father and husband. Words can't fully express my gratitude. I appreciate sharing parenthood, love, and our journey through life with you. I look forward to creating more cherished memories together. I love you.

To my son, Alec Battle-Saunders, you bring so much joy into my life. Being your mom and witnessing you as a father to Amelia fills my heart with happiness. You are an exceptional dad and an incredible son. Your talents are boundless, and I eagerly await to see your dreams unfold. Always remember, you are more than enough; trust yourself, and you are my everything. I love you.

To my daughter, Jayla Logan, I am amazed at the wonderful woman you've become. Your beautiful soul shines as a fantastic mother. I am immensely proud of your achievements and excited to witness your future accomplishments. Having you as my daughter is a true blessing, and you've exceeded all my dreams. I adore you, and I love you.

To my daughter, Kya Logan, you inspire me to continuously grow in my endeavors. Your unwavering support and unconditional love motivate me to be my very best. You are a precious soul, both inside and out. Your unwavering love for God is admirable. Keep sharing your talents with the world. I am so proud of the young lady you have grown into be. I love you.

To my mom, TeJuana Mendoza, I owe who I am to you. Your lessons of honesty and hard work shaped me into the woman I am today. I am in awe of your work ethic and strive to emulate your qualities. Forever grateful for the woman you raised me to be, I hope to make you proud. I love you.

To my readers, thank you for giving my book life and keeping it in circulation. It's my heart's desire that you be motivated, inspired, and empowered to do the seemingly impossible. Cherish every setback and look for the learning lessons to make you more powerful than you could imagine.

About the Author

Meet Jennifer Logan, a remarkable individual whose journey is a true testament to the indomitable spirit that refuses to surrender in the face of challenges. Born with a passion for positive change, Jennifer Logan has navigated life's unexpected twists and turns, emerging stronger and more determined than ever.

From the outset, Jennifer Logan embraced the philosophy of never giving up and standing up for what is right. These principles have become the guiding lights in the journey. It is a journey marked by resilience and an unwavering commitment to the well-being of the people.

The opportunity to represent the community is a profound honor for Jennifer. With humility and dedication, they pledge to be a steadfast advocate for positive change. Jennifer Logan recognizes the power of unity and envisions a future defined by progress and prosperity. The lessons learned from life's challenges serve as a driving force to propel this vision into reality.

In the heart of Jennifer Logan, there is a deep commitment to fostering a better tomorrow for all. The call for unity is not just a rallying cry but a guiding principle that will shape their work. It is a call to harness the collective power of the people to build a legacy of strength and resilience.

As Jennifer Logan embarks on this new chapter, their focus remains on creating a brighter future for everyone. Through tireless efforts and a dedication to the principles of unity, Jennifer

Logan aims to contribute to a legacy that echoes the values of strength, resilience, and progress. In simple delicate terms, Jennifer Logan invites everyone to join hands in building a tomorrow that holds the promise of a better and more prosperous life for all.

Preface

Welcome to the world within the pages of "Ignite," where my journey unfolds, a narrative that bears witness to an unyielding spirit refusing surrender in the face of life's trials.

Life's unexpected challenges have been my greatest teachers, illuminating the resilience and determination that reside within me. As I embark on this path, I carry with me the invaluable lessons of never giving up and the unwavering commitment to fight for what is right.

The opportunity to represent the people in this new chapter deeply honors me. I extend a heartfelt pledge to be an unyielding advocate for positive change. "Ignite" is not just a book; it's a journey we take together. Let's harness the formidable power of unity and chart a course toward a future defined by progress and prosperity.

Within these pages, I invite you to discover the driving force behind my commitment to a better tomorrow. With unity as our guide, we can collectively work toward a legacy marked by strength, resilience, and a brighter future for all. The call to action is not just mine; it's ours.

As you delve into "Ignite," know that each word is an extension of my dedication to tirelessly work toward the vision of a better future. Together, let's turn the narrative of struggle into one of triumph. Let's build a legacy that echoes the principles of strength, resilience, and progress.

So, as we navigate through these pages together, may the story of "Ignite" serve as a reminder that, with determination, unity, and a steadfast commitment to what is right, we can indeed illuminate the path to a better and brighter future.

Contents

Chapter 1: Taking the High Road

"When respect is violated, you can either teach them to do better or allow them to repeat the behavior to someone else."

-Jennifer Logan

Often, life presents us with situations where we are tempted to fight back, to meet our offenders on their level. It's that familiar urge for revenge, the desire for a "tit for tat" response. But as Michelle Obama wisely said, "When they go low, we go high." Revenge may seem sweet at the moment, but it comes at the cost of our character and self-worth.

It was on a day filled with anticipation and nervousness that I found myself caught in such a situation. My employer had organized a pie in the face event to raise money for a children's charity. As I rushed to the store, traveling a long distance, I couldn't help but feel a sense of urgency. I knew I was running late, but I was determined to participate and lend my support to this beautiful cause.

Finally arriving at the store, I was greeted by the sight of a long table adorned with whipped cream and aluminum pans. Thirteen chairs were lined up, occupied by store management and the market team, to which I belonged, supporting the human resources division. My heart raced with a mix of excitement and nerves as I realized I was the last one to arrive.

Walking past my peers and store management, I observed their unrecognizable faces, covered in whipped cream from head to toe. Laughter filled the air as they reveled in the messy delight of the event. An associate motioned for me to keep walking, guiding me to my designated seat. The sight of my colleagues covered in cream only heightened my anxiety, as I had never been pied before. However, I was determined to push past my reservations and participate wholeheartedly.

With a garbage bag tightly wrapped around my body, leaving only my head exposed, I sat down in my designated chair. The restrictive bag limited my movements, adding to my sense of vulnerability. The host, wielding a microphone, surveyed the crowd of approximately 600 associates and asked if anyone wanted to pay to pie me. To my surprise, many heads shook in refusal. But then, from the right side of me, I heard the market manager's voice rise above the rest.

"Pie her now! Pie her now!" He chanted, his words dripping with a mischievous tone. I couldn't help but lean forward, glancing at him in disbelief.

"Really? What have I done to you?" I questioned, my voice laced with a mix of confusion and frustration. The market manager chuckled, seemingly amused by my reaction, and demanded that they hurry up.

As I took my designated seat, a sense of nervous anticipation filled the air. The atmosphere was charged with excitement, and I couldn't help but feel a surge of adrenaline coursing through my veins. Little did I know that this seemingly innocent event would soon take a turn for the worse, testing not only my ability to rise above revenge but also my resilience in the face of betrayal.

The associate, with remorse in her voice, whispered an apology into my ear. "I am so sorry," she said. "He made me do this, and I really did not want to. This is wrong. I am so sorry." Before I could even process their words or respond, a pie was smacked forcefully against my face, catching me completely off guard.

Startled and in shock, I felt a sense of daze wash over me. The world seemed to blur for a moment as I tried to gather my thoughts. But then, as the initial shock subsided, a pungent odor invaded my senses. It was a smell so foul, so disgusting that it made my stomach churn. It was the unmistakable scent of canned fish, "sardines."

Fearful of what I might see, I hesitated to open my eyes. I didn't want to breathe through my nose for fear of inhaling the putrid stench. But I had no choice. I needed to breathe, so I cautiously opened my mouth, only to be met with a sickening combination of sweet cream and oily fishy tuna. It was a revolting mixture that made me gag.

In my attempt to protest, to utter the word "stop," another pie collided with my face, cutting off my words. The impact sent a splattering sound echoing through the air, adding to the humiliation and disbelief I felt. And just when I thought it couldn't get any worse, another pie, this time filled with whipped cream and sardines, smacked me on top of my head. Plop!

Sitting helplessly in my plastic chair, I felt a surge of helplessness and vulnerability. The cream and oil from the sardine pies seeped down my neck, saturating my clothes and leaving an unpleasant residue on my skin. It was a moment of utter defenselessness as the cheers of the crowd seemed to fade into the background.

I sat there, frozen in shock, as the realization sunk in. $20 worth of sardine whipped cream pies had just hit me square in the face. The trash bag I had hastily put on as a shield had done little to protect me from the onslaught of fishy projectiles. I could feel the slimy remnants seeping through the plastic, soiling my clothes, hair, and skin.

As I ripped the trash bag off, my eyes stung from the mixture of cream and fish particles. Blinking away the discomfort, I glanced around at the 600+ associates who were now staring at me. Their expressions ranged from confusion to disbelief as if they couldn't comprehend what had just transpired before their eyes. There were no cheers or applause, only a silence broken by the stifled giggle by Jerry.

Turning to my right, I locked eyes with the market manager. One eye was obscured by a layer of food residue, but I could see the amusement dancing through the other eye. His laughter echoed through the air, and I could hear him muttering about how it was the best $20 he had spent in a long time. Anger, humiliation, and fear surged within me, threatening to bubble over.

But at that moment, I made a conscious decision. I would react with no reaction. I knew that any response I gave would only fuel their amusement further. So, without saying a word, I turned away and swiftly made my way out of the immediate area.

Every step I took left behind a trail of fish bits and whipped cream, a physical reminder of the humiliation I had just endured. I avoided making eye contact with anyone, unable to bear the pity or amusement that I might see in their eyes. My only focus was on escaping, on reaching the sanctuary of my car where I could gather myself in solitude.

The building loomed before me, a massive 200,000 square feet structure that seemed to stretch on forever. It felt like an eternity stood between me and my escape. I quickened my pace, determined to minimize the attention drawn to me. Each step became a desperate plea to blend into the background, to become invisible.

As I entered the receiving area, I was met by three hourly associates. They looked at me with empathy, their eyes filled with genuine concern. They asked if they could help clean me off before I ventured back into the store, offering a towel and some ethnic hair shampoo from off of the store shelf. They explained that they had witnessed the entire incident and felt a deep sympathy for what I had gone through. Their kindness touched me, even in my humiliated state.

At that moment, I didn't want to talk or be in anyone's presence. All I wanted was to escape and retreat to the solace of my home, to piece together the fragments of my shattered dignity. But the associates pleaded with me, their voices filled with sincerity. They insisted that I shouldn't leave in such a state, that they genuinely wanted to help minimize the shame I might face walking through the store covered in fishy mess. Reluctantly, I agreed.

I stood in the dimly lit backroom, surrounded by the lingering scent of detergent and mop water. The water station, typically reserved for the mundane task of cleaning mop buckets, had become an impromptu refuge for me, a place where I could attempt to salvage some semblance of dignity. It was far from ideal, but given the circumstances, the associates had done their best to clean the area to make it somewhat bearable for me.

As I glanced at my reflection in the small, cracked mirror, I couldn't help but notice the weariness etched into my face. My hair, damp from the impromptu cleansing, clung to my forehead and cheeks, offering a momentary respite from the chaos that had unfolded just moments before. The tears welled up in my eyes, surprising even myself as they cascaded down my cheeks, mingling with the remnants of the sardine aroma that clung stubbornly to my clothes and chest.

I mustered a weak smile and thanked the associates for their kindness before making my way back into the store. Every step I took was accompanied by a growing sense of self-consciousness as if the entire world had suddenly turned its gaze upon me. My wet hair and soiled clothes seemed to scream my humiliation to the world, and I couldn't shake the feeling that every passing customer was silently judging me.

The walk through the store felt like an eternity, each department a checkpoint on my journey of shame. From electronics to apparel, from grocery to HBA, I hurried past the aisles, my head held low, desperately trying to avoid eye contact with anyone who might catch a glimpse of my disheveled state. The registers, usually a familiar sight, now felt like a finish line I needed to cross, a hurdle to clear before I could escape this nightmare.

With a newfound urgency, I practically sprinted toward the exit, my heart pounding in my chest. Each second felt like an eternity as I weaved through the crowded aisles, my mind consumed with the single thought of reaching the safety of my car. Finally, as I stepped outside, a wave of relief washed over me. I collapsed into the driver's seat, and the tension in my shoulders released as if a weight had been lifted.

The tears that had been threatening to spill over finally broke free, streaming down my face in a torrent of emotion. I cried uncontrollably, feeling the weight of the day's events crashing down upon me. I felt broken, violated, and utterly defeated. How had it come to this? How had a simple task turned into such a humiliating ordeal?

With a deep breath, I composed myself and wiped away the tears, determined to make it home before my children returned from school. The thought of them seeing me in such a state was unbearable, and I couldn't bear to let them witness the shattered remnants of their mother. Igniting the engine, I embarked on what would prove to be an excruciatingly long commute home.

The minutes stretched into hours, the passing scenery outside my car window becoming a blur. Three hours, which under normal circumstances would have felt like a mere inconvenience, now felt like an eternity. The anger that had simmered beneath the surface began to boil, fueling my determination to leave this nightmare behind me.

As the miles ticked by, I replayed the events of the day in my mind, each replay adding to the mounting fury within me. How could they treat me like that? How could they subject me to such humiliation? The more I dwelled on it, the angrier I became, vowing never to let anyone make me feel so small and insignificant again.

I could feel the anger building up inside me, like a volcano ready to erupt. The events of the day had pushed me to my limit, and I needed some perspective. I grabbed my phone and dialed the numbers of two of my closest peers, Tracy and Howard. They were always there to lend an ear and offer advice when I needed it most.

As the phone rang, my mind raced with thoughts of whether I was just being overly dramatic. Was I overreacting to the situation? Tracy and Howard were both level-headed individuals, and I trusted their judgment.

Finally, Tracy answered the call, her voice filled with concern. I quickly recounted the incident that had left me seething with anger. As I spoke, I could sense the fury in Tracy's voice, matching the rage that was bubbling within me. Howard, too, was equally furious and urged me to take action.

Their reaction validated my feelings and gave me the courage to do something about it. I knew I couldn't let this incident slide. I took a deep breath and made the decision to call my boss and report what had happened.

The phone call with my boss was not what I had anticipated. I explained the situation, hoping for some understanding and support. Instead, I was met with indifference. My boss casually brushed off the incident, reminding me that I had volunteered for the event as if that excused any mistreatment I had endured.

To make matters worse, my boss even chuckled when I mentioned the sardines in the pies. It was as if my pain and disgust were nothing more than a joke to her. I couldn't believe her response or lack thereof. It was clear that she had no sympathy for my feelings, and it left me feeling even more disheartened.

In that moment, I realized that I was on my own. My boss wasn't going to take any action, and I needed to decide how I wanted to handle this situation. I had a choice: to dwell on the abuse and let it consume me or to learn from it and move forward.

Growing up, I had been taught to stand up for myself and not let others disrespect me. I was conditioned to believe that if someone crossed me, I had every right to unleash my anger upon them. It was a behavior that I had grown comfortable with, but deep down, I knew it wasn't the best approach.

As tempting as it was to let my emotions take control and confront my business partner with a fiery outburst, I knew that wouldn't solve anything. It would only make the situation more uncomfortable and escalate the tension. I didn't want to stoop to their level.

Taking a deep breath, I made the conscious decision to keep my composure. I reminded myself that there would be an opportunity to address the events that had taken place, but I needed to approach it with a level head.

It wasn't easy. My humiliation was already at its climax, and every fiber of my being wanted to let my tears and hysterical crying take over, making my hurt, frustration, and embarrassment evident for hundreds of people to see their HR leader devalued publicly. But I knew that wouldn't bring me any closer to a resolution. It would only perpetuate the cycle of negativity.

Instead, I chose to take the high road. I decided to be the bigger person and not let my emotions dictate my actions. It was a difficult decision, but one that I knew I needed to make for my own well-being.

The air in the room felt heavy as I sat down, my heart still racing from the confrontation that had just taken place. I took a deep breath, trying to steady myself before speaking. It was time to have a crucial conversation with my business partner to address the humiliation and disrespect I had experienced.

As I began to explain my feelings, he listened attentively, his eyes filled with a mix of surprise and regret. He assured me that it had never been his intention to make me feel that way, that he had merely been trying to have some fun with a prank that had clearly taken a wrong turn. His words struck a chord within me, and I could sense the sincerity in his voice.

In that moment, I realized that forgiveness was needed for my well-being. I had always prided myself on being strong-willed and standing up for myself, but now I found myself grappling with the idea of letting go of the hurt that could potentially consume me. It felt uncomfortable, almost as if I was betraying myself by considering forgiveness.

Yet, deep down, I knew that holding onto these negative emotions was only poisoning my own soul. It was like ingesting venom and expecting the other person to suffer the consequences. But the truth was, while I was toiling with the memory, he carried on with his life, seemingly unaffected by the weight of his actions.

I had created a victim mentality, replaying the incident over and over in my mind, allowing it to define me. But as I looked into his eyes, searching for any signs of remorse, I realized that forgiving him was not about absolving him of his mistakes. It was about freeing myself from the chains of resentment that were holding me back.

It was a risk, a leap of faith, to believe that forgiveness could truly set me free. But I was willing to take that risk, to break free from the bondage of anger and hurt. And so, I made the decision to forgive him, not for his sake, but for my own.

In that moment, a weight seemed to lift off my shoulders. It was as if a burden I had been carrying for far too long had finally been released. I felt a newfound sense of liberation and freedom to move forward without being shackled to the past.

The growth I experienced through this journey taught me a valuable lesson – that forgiveness is not a weakness but a strength. It takes immense courage to let go of the pain and choose to forgive, especially when it feels easier to hold onto the anger. But in doing so, I reclaimed my power and took control of my own happiness.

I applauded myself for keeping my character intact throughout this challenging ordeal. It would have been so easy to stoop to his level, to retaliate with anger and spite. But I chose the high road, and I was proud of that.

More importantly, I was proud that I didn't hold onto my resistance to forgiveness. I had realized that forgiving him meant

I was not condoning his actions or excusing his behavior. Instead, I was giving myself the gift of peace and the opportunity to heal.

Life is like a journey, and I've learned that not forgiving someone can make it tough. It's like going broke emotionally, silently hurting inside and making everything feel unsettled. This can mess up how we get along with others, our work, and how happy we are. So, it's important to forgive those who hurt us.

But forgiving isn't something we do alone. It's like having a team—a group of friends or coworkers who look out for us. They notice when we're feeling upset and help us get out of those bad feelings. These people get that forgiving is not just a gift to others; it's also a way to help ourselves. In our group, we share our feelings, and forgiving becomes a strength.

Sometimes, though, the hurt goes deep, and it's hard to handle on our own. That's where mentors come in. Mentors are likewise guides who create a safe space for us to talk about our problems. They listen to us, comfort us, and give practical advice on dealing with our emotions.

Talking about our problems, or having "necessary conversations," is crucial for good relationships. Whether it's with a business partner or a close friend at work, we need to be brave and talk about conflicts. Ignoring problems just makes things worse. It's like a poison that can ruin our success.

In these talks, it's essential to be prepared. We start by talking about the specific situation that caused the problem, then explain how it hurt us. It's not about blaming but understanding each other. We end the conversation by asking for a commitment to change and suggesting ways to find common ground. These talks build respect and show how strong our relationships are.

But there are times when it's smarter to stay silent. Not every problem needs a big fight, and sometimes it's better to let things settle. Silence prevents misunderstandings and keeps our relationships safe. It's like taking a break, not giving up.

Navigating my own emotions, I remember quotes that guide me. "I am learning to be whole and free within myself, to acknowledge my brokenness, manifest my own happiness, and succeed and fail gracefully." It's like saying I'm on a journey to be emotionally rich.

I've also learned to treat feelings like visitors—they come and go. It's a skill that helps me handle tough emotions and come out stronger on the other side.

"My viewpoint will either offend the weak-minded or interest a wise person." This reminds me to be real, even if it's not always popular. Being true to myself helps me connect with people who share my values and understand me.

Life is like a play of relationships, and forgiving, having necessary conversations, and sometimes staying silent create a beautiful masterpiece of emotional strength. As I explore myself, guided by mentors and supported by my friends, I embrace the richness of emotional wealth. True success comes from forgiving and building genuine connections with others.

Chapter 2: Lights, Camera and Action

"Use your voice to inspire others, spread kindness, and make the world a better place. Every word you speak holds the power to uplift and empower. Choose them wisely and be the change you wish to see."

-Jennifer Logan

As I embarked on a new challenge, I realized the importance of trusting my process of getting ready. Whether it's tackling new content or displaying my knowledge, having faith in my abilities became crucial. With no room for do-overs, I knew I had to be prepared to seize the opportunity when the big day arrived.

A prime example of this occurred on a manic Monday when my business partner asked if I could accompany Sandra Lee, a renowned chef and author, on a tour of food banks in New York City. Sandra Lee's dedication to supporting Share Our Strength, an organization that aids food banks, made this a unique and valuable opportunity. The catch? I had no prior knowledge of Sandra Lee or any particular interest in cooking. Nevertheless, I agreed to represent my company in their partnership with Share Our Strength.

The night before our first meeting, I was handed six pages of media notes. Perplexed, I inquired about their purpose, only to discover that Sandra Lee's celebrity status often attracted media attention. I was expected to speak as a representative for my company. Initially, the sheer volume of information was daunting, but I knew I had to rise to the occasion.

Trusting my process, I began by studying the media notes. I read through the content, making sure to understand and internalize it. To reinforce my understanding, I practiced delivering the information in front of a mirror. Observing my body language and facial expressions helped me assess my confidence in conveying the content.

Seeking additional input, I reached out to a coworker for their perspective. Their feedback not only boosted my confidence but also provided valuable insights into how I could come across as more assured during the press conferences. Armed with this knowledge, I honed my delivery, ensuring that my message was clear and impactful.

To further reinforce my grasp of the material, I repeatedly wrote down the key points. This technique has always helped me retain information effectively. I also took the initiative to research how others had represented their companies at press conferences. By studying their approaches, I learned to paraphrase and make the message my own, enhancing my confidence in delivering it.

It was essential to strike a balance between personalizing the message and ensuring that the core key facts were not diluted. I carefully selected key phrases and figures to deliver a powerful and memorable message. This approach allowed me to convey the necessary information while infusing my own unique style and personality into the delivery.

The day of our first meeting with food bank organizations arrived, and I felt a mix of excitement and nervousness. However, any apprehension I had about meeting Sandra Lee and establishing rapport with her quickly dissipated as soon as we crossed paths. Instantly, I was drawn to her kind-hearted nature, good spirit, and down-to-earth personality. It was clear that touring with her would be a pleasure and honor.

Before the food bank tour began, Alvin and I had a same-page meeting where Sandra's PR team outlined her expectations and briefed us on the upcoming days. This meeting ensured that we were all well-informed and aligned with the tour's objectives. Being aware of what the tour entailed allowed us to approach each interaction with confidence and clarity.

Our first stop was a roundtable discussion in Long Island, NY, where representatives from various food bank organizations gathered. The purpose was to discuss their reach and the pressing need for support. As each person shared their personal connection to food banks and why this mission was important to them, I couldn't help but feel a sense of vulnerability.

During this exercise, I found myself wishing they would skip me. Memories of a painful portion of my childhood resurfaced, reminding me of the days when I was deprived of food and had nothing to eat. In my formative years in elementary and middle school, I faced an incredibly challenging and heartbreaking situation. My father, grappling with a substance abuse problem, made the devastating choice to prioritize his addiction over taking care of me. As a result, I found myself in a position where the only meals I could rely on were the ones provided at school through the free breakfast and lunch program for underserved children.

For me, school became a refuge, not just for education but also for sustenance. Those meals served as a lifeline, ensuring that I had at least some nourishment during the day. However, as the final school bell rang, signaling the end of the day and the beginning of the long, lonely evenings, a sense of dread would settle over me. I knew that once I left the school grounds, I would not have another meal until the following morning.

The summer months were particularly grueling. With no school to provide those essential meals, I faced the harsh reality of going without food for extended periods. The hunger pangs gnawed at my stomach, a constant reminder of my dire circumstances. It was during these months that the true extent of my predicament became painfully evident.

Desperate to find ways to eat, I would muster up the courage to approach my neighbors, childhood friends who had become my confidants in this tumultuous journey. I would humbly ask if they had any spare food, hoping that they would understand my plight and offer me something to sustain myself. It was a humbling experience, but the kindness and compassion shown by these neighbors provided me with a glimmer of hope in the middle of the darkness.

On occasions when my neighbors were unable to help, I would resort to staying over at my friends' houses. These sleepovers not only provided me with a place to lay my head but also ensured that I would have a meal in my belly. I am forever grateful for the generosity of these friends and their families, who opened their homes and hearts to me when I needed it most.

However, there were times when these options were simply not available to me. It was during these moments of sheer desperation that I experienced the depths of hunger. The emptiness in my stomach mirrored the emptiness I felt in my heart as I longed for the basic necessity of sustenance. The pain and physical weakness that accompanied this prolonged hunger were profound, leaving me feeling utterly defeated and alone.

Eventually, I reached a breaking point. Unable to bear the weight of starvation any longer, I mustered the courage to reach out to my mother. I vividly remember the mix of fear and hope that swirled within me as I confided in her, revealing the harsh reality of my situation. Minutes after I spoke with my mother, my Aunt Vergie called me. She told me to get dressed and come outside. She took me to the grocery store and helped me shop for food, telling me which items went well together when preparing meals. We had a heaping cart of food. Then we went to my house and put the food up. The best part was Aunt Vergie taught me how to cook the food. We made a delicious meal together. I was so relieved that I told my mom that I was starving. She found a way to get me what I needed. My Aunt Vergie was so gracious, loving, and understanding of the circumstance, seeing how I did not have any food in the pantry, refrigerator, or freezer. Well, it was a strangled muskrat in the freezer. The muskrat was choked with all the fur, eyes protruding, and teeth showing. In my most hungry state, I refused to eat that. I would rather knock on the doors of my neighbors and see who would share a meal than eat that rodent.

After Aunt Vergie did what my mom asked her to do, she called her and comforted her, letting her know I was okay.

The next day, when I came home from school, I noticed a crowd of people in our front yard and driveway. My dad loaded his van with the food my mother purchased and sold it all. I was beyond devastated. Food is essential for living. I told my mother my dad sold all of the food. I fantasied all day in school about what I was going to make and came home to an empty pantry, refrigerator, and freezer. I could not continue to live like that. The hunger pains were unbearable. My mother decided to retrieve me and relocate me from Norfolk, Virginia, to Miami, Florida, with her. I really wanted to stay in Virginia. I was going into the 9th grade and was accepted into the School of Arts for high school students and a double major (singing and drawing). However, I understood my mother worked in another state, and this required me to leave.

In her own way, my mother responded to my plea. Recognizing the urgency of the situation, she made arrangements for me to live with her. She had to cut down on traveling so I could live with her again. I only lived with my dad for a year. When I moved in with him, she took a job that required a lot of travel. But this job helped us financially. Before, she was working two or three jobs, struggling to support us as a single parent.

My mother worked really hard to manage everything. This job paid her well, and we didn't have to worry about money anymore. I didn't tell her about the tough situation with my dad and his addiction issues because I knew how important this job was for her and for us. It was her way of getting out of years of financial struggles as a single mom.

She studied and taught herself to pass the exams for a dosimetrist tech position at the power plant. Even though she had to move every school year until my last two years of high school, it gave me a stable living environment with her. I'm grateful for all she did to make our lives better.

The emotions overwhelmed me, and tears welled up in my eyes. Desperately trying to maintain composure, I discreetly wiped my eyes whenever I thought no one was looking. The weight of the sadness hit me all at once, and it became challenging to press through it.

At that moment, when it seemed like it was going to be my turn to share, I made a split-second decision to excuse myself and go to the bathroom. I hoped that by the time I returned, they would have moved on with the agenda, and my turn would be forgotten. I took a few deep breaths, collected myself, and then rejoined the group.

To my surprise, when I returned, they circled back to me, giving me the opportunity to share my thoughts. At that moment, I made a conscious choice not to disclose my personal story. Instead, I decided to focus on the staggering and disheartening statistics regarding hungry children in New York. I conveyed how these numbers were baffling and emphasized Walmart's commitment to partnering with food banks and providing financial assistance to meet the needs of the community.

As I walked into the food bank that day, little did I know that I was about to embark on a whole new journey - one that involved media attention of a magnitude I had never experienced before. Reporters, armed with their audio devices, approached me, eager to capture our conversation. Some even went live, accompanied by a full camera crew, ready to broadcast the event to the world. It was an exhilarating and slightly overwhelming experience, and I couldn't help but feel a mix of excitement and nervousness.

With each encounter, I reminded myself of the importance of this moment. I was not just representing myself but also my company and the community I served. It was crucial for me to make a positive impression and ensure that I did justice to the cause we were promoting. I embraced the assignment wholeheartedly, knowing that I was more than capable of rising to the occasion.

The reporters who engaged in conversations with me, relying solely on their audio devices, didn't intimidate me as much. I felt comfortable sharing my thoughts and insights, knowing that my words would be captured on the local news and aired on the New York Long Island News channel later. However, the butterflies in my stomach fluttered wildly when faced with the live video-taping setup of a news station. The thought of how I would look and present factual information on live TV made my heart race.

I resorted to positive affirmations to calm my nerves, repeating them like a mantra to keep my confidence elevated. But as the bright lights were turned on, glaring into my eyes, I couldn't help but feel momentarily dazed. It was as if I had become a deer caught in headlights, frozen without a clear message to convey. Time seemed to stretch on endlessly, though, in reality, it was only a fleeting second before I realized I had to snap out of it and respond to the reporters' questions.

In that critical moment, I decided to keep my answers at a high level, akin to viewing the situation from 50,000 feet above. While I had pages of talking points prepared, I didn't want to come across as robotic or rehearsed. I wanted my message to flow naturally yet polished, allowing my genuine self to shine through. I knew that authenticity would resonate with the audience far more effectively.

So, I began by sharing the staggering statistics of hunger's impact across New York City. The numbers painted a stark picture of the challenges faced by our community. But I didn't stop there. I also highlighted how Walmart Stores Inc. was committed to addressing this epidemic through philanthropic efforts. It was crucial for me to convey the message that our company genuinely cared about making a difference and giving back to the community we served.

The response I received from my colleagues and associates was overwhelming. They praised the news coverage and expressed their admiration for how I represented our company's commitment to the community. It was an honor and a source of immense pride for me to be used in that capacity. Not only did I gain a new skill and experience, but I also discovered a newfound philanthropic heart within myself.

From that day forward, I made it a personal mission to make meaningful contributions to the community annually. The encounter with the media had opened my eyes to the power of raising awareness and the impact it could have on those in need. I realized that it wasn't just about the words I spoke during that interview; it was about the actions I took afterward to make a tangible difference.

"Rather than focusing on the challenge, focus on the opportunity to showcase your aptitude."

-Jennifer Logan

I still remember the time when I stepped into the massive international job fair in Washington, DC. I couldn't help but feel a mix of excitement and nervousness. Representing my employer at such a prestigious event was a great honor, but it was also my first experience with a large-scale recruiting event. Thousands of potential candidates were expected to attend, and I knew I had to be well-prepared to make a lasting impression.

Having learned from previous job fairs, I understood that simply stating what positions were available and the benefits offered by the company wouldn't be enough. To stand out, I needed to showcase my knowledge and be ready to discuss various topics related to the company. So, in the days leading up to the event, I diligently visited the company website and gathered all the company-vetted facts that were already released to the public. This way, I could confidently speak about the organization without disclosing any confidential information.

I also realized that being well-rounded and aware of the company's presence in the media was crucial. Candidates often wanted to know more than just the basic details; they wanted to understand the company's values, its impact on society, and its future plans. Therefore, I made sure to stay updated on the latest news and social media discussions surrounding the company. This would enable me to engage in meaningful conversations and demonstrate my astuteness and knowledge.

As the job fair commenced, I found myself at my employer's table, surrounded by a constant stream of candidates eager to chat about employment opportunities. The line seemed never-ending, and I couldn't help but notice news crews passing by and filming us. It was a testament to the reputation and desirability of our company, but it also added an extra layer of pressure.

Toward the end of the event, as I was beginning to feel exhausted after seven hours of non-stop interaction, a man approached me, expressing his desire to ask a few questions. Without a moment's hesitation, I agreed to speak with him. However, to my surprise, a news crew suddenly appeared out of nowhere, ready to film me live. The pressure was on, and I hadn't even had a chance to check my appearance after a long day of meetings, greetings, interviews, selling, pitching, and dazzling potential hires.

In moments like these, it's important to hold your head up high, even if you don't feel fully prepared. Confidence can go a long way, and projecting an image of readiness can often be just as effective as being completely prepared. I recalled the wise words of Elizabeth Taylor: "Pour yourself a drink, put on some lipstick, and pull yourself together." While I didn't have any wine to consume at that moment, I embraced the concept. I took a deep breath, straightened my posture, and gathered my thoughts.

With renewed confidence, I dove into the interview. The questions came at me one after another, and I answered them to the best of my ability. Drawing on the knowledge I had acquired through years of working for my employer, I spoke passionately about the company's values, its contributions to society, and its vision for the future. I could see the interviewer's interest growing, and I knew I was making a strong impression.

As the interview came to an end, I felt a sense of accomplishment wash over me. Despite the unexpected live filming and the exhaustion that threatened to dampen my spirit, I managed to showcase my expertise and passion for the company. I had successfully navigated the job fair, leaving a lasting impression on potential candidates and the news crew alike.

As I reflect on my experience at the international job fair in Washington, DC, I can't help but be reminded of the power of mindset and the importance of embracing the possibility of greatness. It is this mindset that propels us forward, generates new opportunities, and prevents us from becoming stagnant.

Throughout the event, I witnessed firsthand how a positive and ambitious mindset can open doors and lead to unexpected successes. It was evident that those who approached each interaction with a belief in their own potential were able to make a lasting impression on both candidates and news crews alike. Their confidence and enthusiasm were contagious, drawing people in and creating a ripple effect of positivity.

In the middle of the chaos and pressure, I realized that I needed to adopt this mindset myself. I needed to shift my focus from the fear of not being fully prepared to the possibility of achieving greatness. Instead of dwelling on my perceived shortcomings, I decided to embrace the challenge and believe in my ability to rise to the occasion.

One action step that helped me in this process was practicing thinking and speaking on my feet. I understood that in high-pressure situations, being able to articulate my thoughts clearly and confidently was crucial. So, I made it a point to research commonly asked questions and prepare answers in advance. This not only helped me feel more prepared but also allowed me to showcase my knowledge and passion for the company.

In hindsight, I realized that there were missed opportunities where I could have shared personal stories that would have resonated with potential candidates. For example, I could have mentioned how our company is renowned for changing the lives of its associates, elevating their pay classes, and creating new opportunities for growth. I could have also shared my own experience with food disparity and how it inspired me to be moved by the work of the food bank. By being prepared to speak about myself and my own journey, I would have been able to connect with candidates on a deeper level and potentially open doors for networking and collaboration.

One valuable takeaway from this experience is the importance of having an elevator speech. This concise and impactful story about oneself can be shared in less than 60 seconds, leaving a lasting impression on anyone who hears it. It allows us to showcase our unique experiences, skills, and passions and can serve as a powerful networking tool in various settings.

Throughout this journey, I found inspiration in the wise words of Sir Winston Churchill: "Fear is a reaction. Courage is a decision." It reminded me that fear is natural, but it is how we choose to respond to it that truly matters. By consciously deciding to be courageous and embracing the possibility of greatness, we can overcome our fears and unlock our full potential.

As I move forward, I am determined to apply these lessons in all aspects of my life. Whether it's in my career, personal relationships, or pursuing new ventures, I will choose courage over fear. I will believe in my own potential and continuously seek opportunities for growth and elevation.

This adventure at the job fair has taught me that by embracing the possibility of greatness, we can create a mindset that propels us forward and opens doors to new opportunities. It is through this mindset that we can prevent stagnation and achieve the success we desire.

And so, armed with the knowledge and experiences gained from this unforgettable event, I am excited to set on my future endeavors with a renewed sense of purpose and a mindset focused on the possibility of greatness. I am ready to take on new challenges, make lasting connections, and continue to grow both personally and professionally.

In my words, "You can be scared, or you can be ready." I choose to be ready.

Chapter 3: Directionally Challenged

"Most problems aren't problems if you stop overthinking."

-Jennifer Logan

In life, we often come across tasks or situations that we are not fond of. They make us uncomfortable, and our instinct is to avoid them at all costs. But what if I told you that by not overcoming these discomforts, we put ourselves at a disadvantage? Let me share a story that taught me the importance of embracing the uncomfortable and thinking my way through challenging situations.

It was a regular day at work when my boss informed me that I had to pick him up from the airport in Northern Virginia. This seemed like a simple enough task, but the thought of it made me uneasy. I wasn't particularly fond of driving in unfamiliar areas, especially during rush hour. However, I knew I couldn't let my discomfort hold me back.

As I prepared for the task, I reminded myself of the principle: "To not overcome puts you at a disadvantage." I realized that if I allowed my fear of driving in traffic to hinder me, I would be limiting my potential and hindering my professional growth. So, I decided to take a different approach. Instead of focusing on what I didn't like, I began to think about the end goal and the role I played in accomplishing it.

The statement, "Be comfortable with being uncomfortable," resonated with me. I understood that growth occurs when we step outside our comfort zones and face our fears head-on. With this mindset, I set off on my journey to pick up my boss from the airport.

I made sure to leave with ample time, hoping to avoid any unnecessary stress. However, as I sat in traffic, my uneasiness started to grow. Minutes turned into what felt like hours, and I couldn't help but worry.

Did my boss miss his flight?

Was his plane delayed?

Doubt began to creep into my mind.

Finally, unable to contain my concern any longer, I decided to call my boss for an update. Little did I know that this phone call would reveal a crucial piece of information that would test my ability to think on my feet.

To my surprise, my boss informed me that he was already at the airport, waiting for me. Confusion washed over me as I assured him that I had been waiting outside. He mentioned a blue hut, which I couldn't see anywhere in sight. It was then that I asked him where exactly he was waiting, assuming he was at the large Dulles Airport.

His response left me speechless. He wasn't at Dulles Airport at all. He was at a private airport, and no one had informed me of the change in plans. My heart sank, realizing that I had made a critical mistake. My teammates had already picked up their bosses, knowing exactly where to find them, while I was left clueless.

At that moment, I had a choice to make. I could let my mistake consume me, or I could embrace the discomfort and find a solution. Remembering the principle and truth statement, I chose the latter.

With a sense of urgency, I asked my boss for the physical address of the private airport. I assured him that I would make my way there as quickly as possible. As I drove toward the private airport, my mind raced with thoughts of how I could have missed this important detail. However, I knew that dwelling on my mistake wouldn't change the situation. I had to focus on the mission at hand – picking up my boss and ensuring his satisfaction.

As I punched the address into my trusty GPS, a wave of panic washed over me. The screen flashed, indicating that I was an hour and a half away from my destination. And to make matters worse, Northern VA was notorious for its traffic jams. I could feel the embarrassment creeping up within me, knowing that I was already running late.

In a desperate attempt to salvage the situation, I called up my peer and asked if he could go back and fetch my boss. However, instead of sympathy, all I received was laughter. My peer couldn't contain his amusement as he informed me that I was probably going to get fired. To add insult to injury, he revealed that my boss had already arrived at his location and was busy touring with his own boss.

Feeling a sinking feeling in the pit of my stomach, I finally arrived at what my GPS claimed was the airport. But as I looked around, I couldn't see any resemblance to the bustling airport I had imagined. Instead, there were numerous small buildings scattered across vast stretches of land. It was anything but the typical airport scene.

With a heavy heart, I dialed my boss once more, hoping he could provide me with some much-needed guidance. The call was filled with dread, as I knew I had no other choice but to reach out for help. When I asked him for more information, all he could offer was that it was a blue building. My heart sank further as the majority of the buildings I saw were indeed blue. It seemed like I had hit another dead end.

Frustrated and lost, I spent another agonizing hour searching for my boss. It felt like an eternity, with every passing minute intensifying my anxiety. And then, finally, I spotted him. There he was, standing on a patch of gravel, his coat looped through his luggage, positioned in front of him. I pulled up beside him, relief washing over me.

As soon as my boss got into the car, I couldn't help but repeatedly apologize. I was overwhelmed by the embarrassment and shame of getting lost in an unfamiliar place. But to my surprise, my boss didn't let me dwell on those negative emotions. He knew that I was already beating myself up, so he swiftly changed the subject, sparking a conversation about something entirely unrelated.

In that moment, I realized that my boss understood the weight of my embarrassment. He didn't want me to wallow in it but rather move on from the mishap and focus on the task at hand. His compassion and ability to lighten the mood was a welcome relief, and it helped me transition from my unhappy state to a more positive mindset.

As I reflected on the chaotic events of that day, one thing became abundantly clear: fact-gathering is crucial. I had made the mistake of assuming that a simple address plugged into my GPS would be enough to get me to my destination. But boy, was I wrong.

You see, I've always had a tendency to get lost easily. Navigating unfamiliar streets while driving has never been my strong suit. And yet, I had failed to gather all the necessary information I needed to plan this trip effectively. It was a recipe for disaster waiting to happen.

In hindsight, I realized that I should have taken the time to do a test run of the route before the actual day of the trip. By familiarizing myself with the roads and landmarks, it wouldn't have felt like such a foreign journey. But in my eagerness to get everything done, I had neglected this crucial step.

Sure, I had relied on my trusty GPS to guide me. But the truth is, even with the GPS, I still managed to get lost. It became clear to me that a GPS alone was not enough to navigate through unfamiliar territory. I needed to be proactive and take charge of my own direction.

Another factor contributing to my predicament was my discomfort with driving in areas I had never been to. It was a fear of the unknown, a fear of getting lost and feeling helpless. And so, I had often found ways to avoid driving in unfamiliar areas, thinking that it would save me from the embarrassment and frustration of getting lost.

However, as I reflected on this experience, I realized that by avoiding what I wasn't comfortable with, I was only stifling my own development. How could I expect to grow and learn if I constantly shied away from challenging situations? It was a valuable lesson that I needed to embrace.

From that day forward, I made a promise to myself. I vowed to step out of my comfort zone and face the challenges head-on. I knew that it wouldn't be easy, but I understood the importance of growth and self-improvement. After all, how could I expect to navigate through life successfully if I couldn't even navigate the streets?

Talking about my comfort zone, there was a time when I stood at the edge of the dodgeball court. My heart pounded with a mix of nerves and excitement. I had never played the game before, but here I was, about to embark on a new adventure. I had studied the players' guide, trying to wrap my head around the rules and regulations, but the overwhelming feeling made me want to back out. Yet, I knew backing out would leave our team short-handed and possibly disqualified. So, I gathered my courage and decided to take the leap. After all, this was a fundraising event to help those with MS.

Our team, aptly named the Nor'easters, was competing in a championship event held in a massive convention center. Six teams battled it out, and the stakes were high. We had spent weeks raising money for a cause close to our hearts, multiple sclerosis, and this was the pinnacle of our efforts. The arena was packed with thousands of spectators eagerly awaiting the games to unfold.

As I stepped onto the court, my nerves threatened to consume me. Every fiber of my being screamed at me to run away, to escape the impending embarrassment. But I couldn't let my team down. I couldn't be the first one to get out; I had to prove to myself that I was capable of taking on this challenge.

With a plan in mind, I decided to use my agility and the advantage of my shorter stature. I would run in a loop, seeking refuge behind my taller teammates. I also made a conscious choice not to rush and grab balls immediately. Instead, I would wait for an opportune moment, letting the game come to me.

As the referee's whistle pierced the air, I found myself in a whirlwind of confusion. I focused on protecting my face and sought solace in the presence of my teammates. But before I knew it, I was the last player standing on our team. Panic washed over me as I looked at my teammates, pleading for help with my eyes. How had it come to this? The opposing team had a few players left, and I was alone in the face of their fury.

The whistle blew, and a storm of dodgeballs hurtled toward me. I felt paralyzed, unable to move. I dodged, ducked, and weaved, desperately trying to evade the onslaught. It felt like I was a cat chasing its tail, frantically running around to escape the relentless assault. Fear gripped me, making it difficult to pick up a ball and join the offensive.

Eventually, the rest period came, and I took a moment to catch my breath. My teammates looked at me with a mix of confusion and concern. I must have looked like a disheveled mess with one sock near my kneecap, the other fallen to my ankle, and my clothes askew. But deep down, I knew I had to gather my courage and continue fighting.

Returning to the court, I hoped for a miraculous malfunction of the referee's whistle. But my wishful thinking was shattered as the loud blast signaled the resumption of the game. The opposing team was determined to take me down, and their balls flew toward me with unwavering precision.

Then, it happened. WHACK! Lance threw the winning shot, where the ball smacked me on the side of my face, jolting me out of my fear-induced trance. Strangely enough, it was almost a relief. The torment was over, and I could finally breathe again.

As an introvert who preferred to blend into the background only sometimes, being the center of attention in a game I barely understood wasn't exactly my idea of fun. But when it was all said and done, I felt an overwhelming sense of relief. I had faced my fears head-on and survived. I had stepped outside my comfort zone and embraced a new experience. This is one of the most rewarding volunteer fundraising events I ever did. I was challenged to do something unfamiliar and did it extremely well. I am proud to say I was the last one standing, and the team against me had to work hard to get me out. If I had a chance to do this again, I would, and it would be exactly how I experienced it.

As I sit here, reflecting on the many stressful situations I have encountered in my life, I can't help but feel a sense of gratitude for the valuable lessons they have taught me. Stress has a way of consuming our thoughts and clouding our judgment, but I have learned that by following a simple set of steps, we can regain control of our mindset and navigate through even the most challenging situations.

Step 1: Define the Issue

The first step in overcoming stress is to clearly define the issue at hand. Take a moment to identify what exactly is causing you stress. Is it a deadline at work? A conflict with a loved one? By pinpointing the root cause, you can begin to address it head-on.

Step 2: Identify the Impact

Next, consider who may be impacted by the situation and how. Understanding the potential consequences of your actions or decisions allows you to approach the situation with empathy and consideration for others. This awareness helps you make more informed choices.

Step 3: Seek Possible Solutions

Once you have a clear understanding of the issue and its impact, it's time to brainstorm possible solutions. Don't limit yourself to the first idea that comes to mind; instead, explore various options and consider different perspectives. This step allows you to tap into your creativity and find innovative ways to tackle the problem.

Step 4: Make a Decision

After considering the various solutions, it's time to make a decision. Trust yourself and your judgment. Remember, there is no right or wrong answer; it is only what feels most aligned with your values and goals. Take a deep breath and trust that you have the ability to make the best choice for yourself and those around you.

Step 5: Take Action

Now that you have made a decision, it's time to take action. Don't let fear or doubt hold you back. Embrace the opportunity to step outside your comfort zone and face the challenge head-on. Remember, growth and progress often come from pushing through our fears.

Step 6: Check Your Progress

As you move forward, periodically check your progress. Are you on track to achieve your desired outcome? If not, don't be discouraged. Go back to step 3 and recalibrate. It's okay to adjust your approach or seek additional support if needed. The key is to keep moving forward, learning from each experience along the way.

Step 7: Accomplish the Task

Finally, celebrate your accomplishments. You have successfully navigated through a stressful situation, and that deserves recognition. Take a moment to acknowledge your resilience and the lessons you have learned. Review your process and identify areas where you could have done things differently for a smoother transition.

In the words of Confucius, "Life is really simple, but we insist on making it complicated." By following these simple steps, we can simplify our approach to stress and fear. Remember, fear has the power to either paralyze us or propel us toward our goals. The difference lies in our belief in our own capabilities.

As Mandy Hale wisely said, ***"Have faith in your journey. Everything had to happen exactly as it did to get you where you're going next!"*** Embrace the challenges, face your fears, and trust in your ability to overcome them. You are capable of more than you can imagine.

Stress and fear may try to overpower our mindset. Still, by defining the issue, considering the impact, seeking solutions, making decisions, taking action, checking progress, and accomplishing the task, we can regain control and navigate through any situation. Keep it simple, trust in yourself, and remember that every experience is an opportunity for growth.

Chapter 4: Don't be Stingy

"Be patient and embrace your journey."

-Jennifer Logan

As I walked into the busy Women's Symposium in New York City, I got really excited. The room was filled with energetic women who were eager to learn and grow in their jobs. I didn't know that this day would turn into a special mentorship experience for me.

The symposium had different sessions to teach attendees about professional development. I felt honored to be chosen as a mentor for the speed mentoring panel. It meant I could share my professional life lessons.

The symposium started, and I saw many motivated faces with unique stories. The room felt like a place where mentorship could really make a difference. The first session focused on important lessons, setting the stage for the mentoring that was about to happen.

The idea of inspiring people was on my mind as I waited for the people I would be mentoring. The saying, ***"Go soar and be the wind beneath the wings for someone else,"*** was in my thoughts, guiding the experience.

As people went through the different sessions, I noticed the variety of backgrounds and jobs they came from. It showed me that mentorship can connect people from different walks of life. I knew there were stories to be heard and dreams to support in this diverse group.

When it was time for the mentoring sessions, I welcomed my mentees with a friendly smile, excited to learn about their professional journeys. Each conversation was like a unique story with dreams, challenges, and goals. I listened carefully, not just with my ears but with my heart, as they shared their hopes and struggles.

One person, a young professional, stood out. She had a strong determination and spoke about her journey, the problems she faced, and her dreams. It was clear she was ready to do great things but needed some support.

I connected her story to the main idea of this journey—using our skills to help others grow and handle tough situations. As I shared my experiences, the good and bad parts of my career, I saw a spark of inspiration in her eyes.

Our mentoring session became a sharing of wisdom, a nice exchange of ideas, and encouragement. I realized being the wind beneath someone's wings wasn't about telling them what to do. It was about giving them confidence and guidance and making sure they knew they weren't alone.

In those 45 minutes, we talked about how she could grow, face challenges, and celebrate her achievements. The connection we made in that room was more than just about jobs; it was a human connection, a reminder of how much we can impact each other's lives.

I remember the moment I accepted the assignment, feeling a mix of excitement and trepidation. As someone who is always eager to broaden my horizons, I knew that this stretch assignment would provide me with an opportunity to grow.

However, alongside that enthusiasm, fear and uncertainty began to creep into my mind.

Doubts started swirling around, questioning whether I was well-versed enough to handle the task I had agreed to take on. But, instead of allowing those fears to consume me, I made a conscious decision to arrest those negative thoughts and replace them with positive affirmations. I reminded myself that I was capable and that I could do it.

You see, I have never been the type of person who thrives in social situations. I have always been more comfortable keeping to myself, preferring the quiet solitude of my own thoughts. But I knew that in order to break free from the brainwashing thought of being an introvert, I needed to intentionally step out of my comfort zone.

So, I intentionally agreed to this assignment, knowing that it would force me to confront my reservations and challenge myself. I understood that the more I exposed myself to events and activities that pushed me out of my comfort zone, the more comfortable I would become in similar situations in the future. My goal was to have a paradigm shift, redefine my limitations, and expand my comfort zone.

As I embarked on this journey, I quickly realized that it was not going to be an easy one. The discomfort was palpable, and my initial instinct was to retreat back into my shell. However, I knew that in order to grow, I had to push through the discomfort and embrace the unknown.

I found myself standing in front of a room filled with approximately 30 women. It was an incredible opportunity for me to make a difference in their lives, to help them sharpen their core competencies and achieve their career goals. The energy in the room was palpable, and I was ready to dive into this mentoring session headfirst.

As I began the first encounter, I felt a surge of confidence coursing through my veins. Gone were the nerves and uncertainties that had plagued me in the past. I was fully present, exuding confidence and determination. I started by asking probing questions, eager to understand the purpose behind each woman's participation in this session.

Drawing from my experience of helping thousands of employees pursue their career aspirations, I shared insights and strategies that could help these women secure a job, ace an interview, and gain more confidence in their professional journey. The room buzzed with anticipation as we delved into discussions, exploring various techniques and approaches that could position them for promotions and success.

Throughout the session, I witnessed incredible transformations taking place. Women who had initially appeared hesitant or unsure began to embrace their strengths and believe in their abilities. It was a privilege to witness their growth, to see them shed self-doubt and step into their power.

As the day progressed, I couldn't help but reflect on the valuable takeaways that emerged from our interactions. One woman emphasized the importance of patience and embracing the journey. She reminded us that success doesn't happen overnight, but rather, it is a result of perseverance and continuous learning.

Another powerful quote that resonated with me came from Curiano, who likened life to a game. We could choose to play it safe and remain good, or we could take a chance and strive for greatness. This reminder encouraged us to step outside our comfort zones, embrace challenges, and pursue our dreams fearlessly.

An anonymous quote struck a chord with many of the women in the room. It highlighted that the quickest way to acquire self-confidence is by facing our fears head-on. It reminded us that growth and self-assurance come from doing exactly what we are afraid of, pushing past our limitations, and realizing our true potential.

Throughout the session, these quotes served as guiding lights, inspiring us to step into our own power and make a difference in our lives and the lives of others. They reminded us of the importance of service and the impact it can have on our own personal growth. As Mahatma Gandhi once said, "The best way to find yourself is to lose yourself in the service of others." By helping others, we not only brighten their paths but also illuminate our own.

Kush Wisdom also shared a thought-provoking quote that resonated deeply. It encouraged us to focus on loving ourselves rather than seeking validation from others. This reminder reminded us to prioritize self-care, self-acceptance, and self-love, knowing that they are the foundation for building confidence and happiness.

Finally, Buddha's profound words reminded us of the power of kindness and compassion. By lighting a lamp for someone else, we not only brighten their path but also illuminate our own. It is through acts of service and support that we find fulfillment and purpose.

As the mentoring session drew to a close, I couldn't help but feel a sense of fulfillment and gratitude. It was an honor to be a part of these women's journeys and to witness their growth and transformation. The day had been filled with powerful conversations, shared learnings, and a collective commitment to stepping into our greatness.

One day, as I sat at my desk, sifting through the countless emails that flooded my inbox, one subject line caught my eye — "Contest." My heart skipped a beat, for I have always been a competitive person, and any opportunity for work fun was right up my alley. My curiosity piqued, and I eagerly clicked on the email and opened the attached document.

It was a pin design contest held within our company, and the winner would have their pin distributed at the next shareholders' meeting. Instantly, my creative juices started flowing, and I knew I had to participate. With determination in my heart, I set out to design the perfect pin.

Weeks went by, and I poured my heart and soul into creating a pin that would stand out from the rest. Finally, the day arrived when I submitted my design, feeling a mix of excitement and nervousness. Little did I know that saying yes to this adventure would lead to an unexpected reward.

A few days later, as I was engrossed in my daily tasks, an email from the contest organizers appeared in my inbox. My heart raced as I read the words, "Congratulations! You are the winner of the pin design contest!" I couldn't believe it. A wave of elation washed over me, knowing that my creativity had been recognized.

But the reward didn't end there. As a token of appreciation, I was invited to have lunch with our Senior Vice President for Human Resources. The thought of sitting down with such a high-ranking executive sent a surge of anxiety through me. I am an introvert by nature, and the idea of engaging in small talk with someone so important made me uneasy.

In the days leading up to our lunch, I meticulously prepared myself. I studied my business data, memorized statistics, and analyzed quarterly plans. I wanted to make a good impression to show that I was a valuable asset to the company. But despite my thorough preparation, I couldn't help but feel a knot of nervousness in my stomach.

As the day of the lunch approached, my anxiety reached its peak. My hands became clammy, and the room suddenly felt suffocatingly hot. I knew I needed a moment to gather myself. Excusing myself, I hurriedly made my way to the bathroom, hoping to find solace in its quiet confines.

In those few minutes alone, I took a deep breath and reminded myself of a verse from Proverbs that had always brought me comfort – "Trust in and rely confidently on the Lord with all your heart and do not rely on your own insight or understanding." The words echoed in my mind, calming my racing thoughts and alleviating my nervous symptoms.

The time had come. I arrived at the Vice President's office ten minutes early, knowing that in the world of business, punctuality was crucial. To my delight, she was already there, wearing a beaming smile that stretched from ear to ear. Her warmth and genuine excitement to have lunch with me instantly put me at ease.

As we exchanged greetings, she asked where I wanted to go for lunch. Without hesitation, I suggested the café located within the headquarters building. However, to my surprise, she recommended that we take our food to her office to eat versus eating in the cafeteria. Curiosity piqued, I followed her into her office, wondering what our conversation would entail.

As we settled into our seats, I prepared myself for a discussion about business metrics and performance. But to my surprise, she didn't dive into those topics right away. Instead, she asked a simple question that caught me off guard – "Who are you?" She wanted to know my story beyond the confines of my professional life.

I shared personal details about my family, my hobbies, and my interests. In turn, she opened up about her own life, sharing stories that made her relatable and human. In that moment, I realized that this lunch was not just about business; it was an opportunity for us to connect on a personal level.

Over the course of our two-hour power hour, I soaked in the wisdom that the Vice President imparted. One of the first lessons she shared was that success is not achieved by accident. She emphasized the importance of hard work and dedication in reaching her current position. It was a reminder that we must actively pursue our goals and make deliberate choices to shape our careers.

She also stressed the significance of investing in oneself. She recounted how she made the decision to continue her education, recognizing that it would make her more marketable in the ever-evolving business landscape. Her story served as a powerful reminder that personal growth and development are essential ingredients for success.

The topic then shifted to the delicate balance between work, health, family, and personal well-being. We shared stories of the challenges we faced in managing all aspects of our lives. It was comforting to know that even someone in such a high-ranking position had experienced similar struggles.

The Vice President emphasized the importance of self-care and not neglecting one's own needs. She spoke passionately about finding time for oneself in the middle of the chaos of everyday life. It was a lesson I needed to hear, as I often found myself neglecting self-care in favor of tending to other responsibilities.

However, perhaps the most impactful lesson she shared was the importance of loving oneself and disregarding the negative talk that surrounds us. She recounted instances where she faced criticism and judgment from others. Despite the external noise, she stayed true to herself and her aspirations, refusing to let the opinions of others hinder her path to success.

As our conversation came to an end, I couldn't help but feel inspired by the Vice President's wisdom. She had faced adversity and overcame it with grace and determination. Her stories served as a reminder that growth often comes from stepping outside of our comfort zones.

At that moment, I recalled two quotes that resonated deeply with me. The first, by Brian Tracey, reminded me that growth requires embracing discomfort and awkwardness. The second, by Caroline Myss, encouraged me to choose the path that scares me the most, for it is on that path that true growth lies.

Before parting ways, the Vice President shared one final quote by Robert Ingersoll – "We rise by lifting others." This simple yet profound statement served as a guiding principle for her leadership style. It reminded me of the importance of supporting and uplifting those around us, for it is through collective growth that we can achieve greatness.

As I walked away from that lunch, I carried with me a renewed sense of purpose and a deeper understanding of what it takes to succeed. The Vice President had not only shared her experiences and wisdom but had also shown me the power of genuine connection and vulnerability.

From that day forward, I vowed to continue saying yes to new adventures, even if they made me feel uncomfortable. I understood that it is in those moments of vulnerability and growth that we discover our true potential.

So, my dear reader, I encourage you to embrace discomfort, invest in yourself, and prioritize self-care. Surround yourself with those who uplift and support you, and never let the judgments of others deter you from your path to success. Remember, we rise by lifting others, and by doing so, we can create a world where everyone has the opportunity to thrive.

Chapter 5: All that Mental Anguish for Nothing!

"Worrying is a thief of serenity, stealing your peace and yielding nothing in return."

*-Jennifer Logan*When my business partner approached me with an emergency, asking if I could fill in for him at an important business meeting, a wave of fear and doubt washed over me. The meeting, scheduled for Monday, involved presenting to high-level leaders, including my partner's boss, his boss's boss, and all of his peers and support teams for the NE Region. The topic at hand was the total performance of our billion-dollar business in the market – a subject I did not think I was well-versed in.

As I received the PowerPoint deck containing a daunting 98 slides, panic threatened to consume me. How could I possibly absorb all this information and present it effectively to a room full of experienced professionals? I was accustomed to handling human resources matters, leaving the operational aspects to the ops experts. The thought of diving into uncharted territory made me question my abilities and consider backing out.

However, I firmly believed in following through on commitments. I knew that underestimating myself would only hold me back from reaching my full potential. So, despite my fear, I made the decision to face this challenge head-on. I resolved to study the content as much as possible and asked questions to ensure I had a clear understanding of the material provided.

Some might argue that simply reading the slides would suffice, considering the circumstances. After all, everyone was aware that I was stepping in at the last minute. However, as a skilled facilitator, I knew that merely regurgitating the information on the slides would not engage the audience or convey the message effectively. I wanted to make a positive, lasting impression, even though I was just filling in.

With this mindset, I dedicated the next 24 hours to immersing myself in the material. I devoured each slide, absorbing every piece of information, and started to piece together a cohesive narrative in my mind. I wanted to understand the facts and figures and the underlying story behind our business's performance in the market.

As I delved deeper, I realized that this exposure assignment was an opportunity for growth. It pushed me out of my comfort zone and forced me to expand my knowledge and skills. Rather than letting fear take over me, I chose to embrace the unknown and transform it into a chance to prove myself.

As I stood at the private airport, waiting to board the company jet with the Northeast vice president and the rest of the team, my anxiety reached new heights. The short notice had left me unable to arrange a flight, and now I was faced with the prospect of flying alongside high-ranking executives. The mere thought of it made my knees tremble and my heart race.

I had always been a nervous flyer, but this situation took my fear to a whole new level. Butterflies, caterpillars, and even maggots seemed to have taken residence in my stomach, churning and wriggling with unbelievable anxiety. Every possible scenario played out in my mind, each one more terrifying than the last.

Questions bombarded me relentlessly. What if they asked me something I didn't know? Did I need to study more information before boarding the plane? The uncertainty gnawed at me, fueling my already overwhelming apprehension. It felt as though my mind was going in a thousand different directions, and I was struggling to keep up.

The toll of this relentless anxiety was evident in my physical and emotional state. Nail-biting became a habit, a manifestation of the stress that consumed me. I lost five pounds from not eating, and sleep eluded me as my mind raced with worries and doubts. I became irritable and snappy, unable to find solace or peace of mind.

In the midst of this mental turmoil, I had to remind myself of the truth: I had faced challenges before and emerged stronger. I couldn't let fear paralyze me, especially when it came to fulfilling my commitments. It was time to confront my anxieties head-on and find a way to navigate through the turbulence of my mind.

I had never been on a jet before, and the thought of it made me excited but also incredibly nervous. My mind was racing with questions and concerns. Would there be a lot of turbulence? Would I be comfortable in my seat, or would I have to squeeze myself in and suck in my belly? Will my motion sickness go rampant? Will my ears pop now? I had all these thoughts and more as I embarked on this journey.

As I arrived at the airport, I was relieved to find that parking was easy and conveniently close to the entrance. I didn't have to worry about checking my bags or showing a ticket either. The whole process seemed surprisingly simple and straightforward. I made my way toward the sitting area and immediately noticed the presence of not only the members of the regional team but also the divisional team. It was unexpected to see so many familiar faces there. This trip had been arranged at the last minute, and I'm sure the look on my face gave away my nervousness. I was scared to death, to say the least.

However, to my surprise, a few leaders from the leadership team approached me with warm greetings. They sensed my anxiety and consciously kept the conversation light, avoiding any business-related topics. Their approach instantly helped alleviate my fear and anxiety. At that moment, I had a teachable moment. I realized I needed to relax and not get worked up over things. I needed to shift my attention away from stress and focus on matters that would keep me calm.

I arrived in Ohio feeling a mix of excitement and nervousness. After checking into the hotel, I wasted no time and pulled up the presentation I had been working on. I knew I had to make the most of this opportunity, so I decided to focus my attention on the subjects that I had the least experience with.

Feeling the need for validation, I called up my business partner and asked him to listen to me rehearse each slide. He was a numbers guru and knew the business inside out. He could sense my stress and overthinking and didn't hesitate to push me. He gave me tough coaching in those moments of despair, urging me to get it together. And I needed that. Those harsh words served as a reminder to stay focused on the task at hand.

I studied the content relentlessly, going through it until the early hours of the morning. Sleep eluded me, but I couldn't afford to let exhaustion get in the way. The meeting was scheduled to start at 8 am, and I had to be prepared. With my materials in hand, I made my way toward the meeting room.

However, before entering, I took a detour to the bathroom. The stress had taken its toll on me, and I found myself vomiting. Staring at my reflection in the mirror, I couldn't help but feel pathetic. The weight of the pressure I had put on myself had made me incredibly sick. In that vulnerable moment, I whispered to myself, "Jesus, take the wheel."

One particular Biblical reference came to mind, giving me a supernatural strength to face the challenge before me. I remembered Philippians 4:6-7, which reminded me not to be anxious but to pray with thanksgiving. The promise of God's incomprehensible peace guarding my heart and mind in Christ Jesus gave me the courage to keep going. I washed my face, gargled to freshen my breath, and gathered my things from the floor. With my head held high, I walked into the meeting room.

To my surprise, all the seats were taken, and I found myself squeezed in between the Regional VP and the Divisional VP on the front row. Despite this, I remained unphased. I had acquired a newfound confidence through prayer and standing on the biblical verse. I truly believed I was going to get the job done.

My Regional VP noticed my arrival and asked if I was okay and ready to present. With conviction, I responded, "Yes, sir." I got up and was ready to speak to 98 slides. For my comfort, I had notes in hand and scribbled down for reference. As I started presenting,

I decided not to rely on those notes. I knew the material inside out and was determined not to get stuck on any part of the presentation. As I began to speak, I realized I had a complete understanding of the entire business operation. It was reflective as I delivered the presentation; I did not have to read the slides, and I used them as a trigger for what to discuss.

I confidently spoke about all facets of the billion-dollar business, covering topics such as Membership, Fresh Operations, HR, Health and Wellness, Loss Prevention, Competition, Sales, Profit, and our strategies to meet enterprise objectives. Throughout my presentation, I received cues from my NE VP, who smiled, gave me a WOW face, and even presented a thumbs up. Glancing around the room, I could see shocked faces. I had their attention, and many were in disbelief at how well I was able to speak to the intricacies of the business.

As my session ended, it was time for the Q&A portion. I had anticipated that I wouldn't receive many questions since I was filling in for someone else. However, to my surprise, they fired off questions left and right. Yet, amazingly, I was able to answer every inquiry with confidence. My newfound confidence remained unshaken.

During the first break, I was overwhelmed by the amount of positive feedback I received. People approached me, expressing how awesome they thought I was. It was a validation that all the hard work and preparation had paid off.

As I reflected on my successful presentation, a realization hit me like a bolt of lightning. I had been working with the everyday aspects of the business, listening to tour notes, and attending weekly staff meetings. Without realizing it, I had absorbed a wealth of knowledge about the global business. I knew more than I had given myself credit for. I am also forever grateful to Mohammed for trusting me to represent him and our market. He had me practice the night before, and he fussed at me. He said I was in my head for no reason, and I could do this. He was right. I was fortunate to have a Market Manager who rooted for me and saw the potential in my capabilities before I knew myself. Mohammad Khan and Casey Usumani were awesome Market Managers who pushed me to learn business operations beyond HR.

ThIs "ah ha" moment was a turning point for me. I realized that I had put myself through unnecessary mental torment leading up to the presentation. I had doubted my abilities and allowed fear to consume me. But now, with the successful completion of the task, I saw that my fears had been unfounded.

I made a firm decision to incorporate positive affirmations into my daily routine. I understood the power of shifting my thoughts into a positive realm. Short but powerful statements like "I can and I will," "Not today, devil... you have no authority over me," and "The only person that can stop your dreams is you" became my mantras. By repeating these affirmations, I conditioned my mind to believe in my own capabilities and to banish any negative thoughts that threatened to sabotage my success.

Another important takeaway from this experience was the realization that making mistakes is okay. In many cases, the audience doesn't even notice a mistake. And if it is an identifiable mistake, I learned not to dwell on it. Instead, I embraced the ability to laugh it off and keep moving forward. Mistakes are part of the learning process, and I refused to let them hold me back. Either you win, or you're learning a lesson.

I also understood the power of conditioning my mind to believe in desired outcomes. Instead of feeding my mind with fears and negative "what ifs," I redirected that energy toward envisioning myself as successful in all my endeavors. I realized that negative thinking only served to sabotage my own potential. By focusing on positive thoughts and visualizing success, I was able to manifest positive outcomes.

In this journey of self-discovery, I came across two quotes that resonated deeply with me. The first was from Dr. Spock, who wisely said, "Trust yourself. You know more than you think you do." These words served as a reminder that I possessed the knowledge and skills to overcome any challenge. I just needed to trust in myself.

The second quote, by Sarah Bareilles, urged me to show the world how big my bravery was. It reminded me that bravery wasn't the absence of fear but rather the ability to push through it and take risks. I realized I had the strength within me to face any obstacle head-on.

With these newfound insights and the power of positive affirmations, I embarked on a journey of self-belief and self-assurance. I knew that I had the ability to achieve greatness, and I refused to let doubt hold me back. The Ohio presentation was just the beginning of a new chapter in my life, one where I would embrace my own power and confidently pursue my dreams.

Chapter 6: Get Ready You're It!

"Complacency robs you of the chance to live a truly fulfilling and rewarding life."

*- Jennifer Logan*We all have our comfort zones, those familiar spaces where we feel secure and confident. It's natural to want to stay within these boundaries, as they provide us with a sense of stability and control. However, there comes a time when stepping outside of our comfort zone becomes necessary for personal growth and development.

The comfort zone is a double-edged sword. While it offers us a sense of security, it can also limit our potential and hinder our progress. When we are too comfortable, we tend to become complacent and resistant to change. We may fear failure or rejection, and as a result, we shy away from taking on new challenges. However, by staying within our comfort zones, we miss out on valuable opportunities for growth and self-improvement.

While the benefits of stepping outside of our comfort zones are clear, it's important to acknowledge the fear and resistance that often accompany such endeavors. Fear of failure, rejection, or the unknown can hold us back from taking the leap. However, it's crucial to remember that growth only occurs outside of our comfort zones. We must adopt a "get over it and get it done" mindset to overcome these fears.

I had been selected to attend a training class at the home office, a great opportunity for personal and professional growth. I reviewed the travel plans, eager to see who I would be traveling with from the airport to the hotel and who would be in charge of transporting us around during our week-long stay.

However, as I glanced at my phone, a notification caught my attention. It stated that I had been appointed as the group's designated driver. Panic instantly surged through my veins, causing a mental heart attack. I couldn't believe my luck. Why me? I wondered.

At that moment, my mind raced, desperately searching for a way out of this responsibility. I concocted a list of 30 reasons why one of the other passengers should replace me as the driver. I hoped that someone would step forward and save me from this daunting task. After all, I had never driven a 15-passenger van before, nor had I ever driven a car that held more than four people. I felt completely unprepared and unsafe to take on this role.

Nevertheless, I reluctantly approached the rental counter and retrieved the keys since the van had been booked under my name. The weight of the responsibility settled heavily on my shoulders as I awaited the arrival of the group. Once we were all gathered together and ready to leave, I mustered up the courage to ask who would be driving, dangling the keys in front of them, hoping someone would take them from my outstretched hand. To my surprise, no one volunteered.

In a desperate attempt to elicit a reaction, I decided to play the role of a drama queen. I allowed my emotions to rise internally, producing watery eyes and a slight tremble. I thought surely someone would be moved by my dramatics and offer to take the wheel. But to my dismay, this group remained unfazed by my self-inflicted torment.

Realizing that my theatrics were not getting me anywhere, I shifted my approach. I decided to appeal to their sense of safety and concern. I disclosed that I had never driven a 15-passenger van before, emphasizing that my experience was limited to cars that held no more than four people. I wanted them to understand that they would not be safe with me as their driver.

Yet, despite my plea, no one seemed willing to take on the responsibility. It was clear that I had no choice but to face my fears head-on and become the driver for this journey.

As I stood there, listening to the passenger's remark about transporting more than four people, I couldn't help but feel a sense of disbelief. It was clear that I was not prepared for the comeback that followed. The group's response, however, was unanimous - no one seemed nervous about my driving abilities or the prospect of being uncomfortable.

Confusion and frustration began to bubble within me. Why were they so calm and nonchalant about this? Did they not realize how uncomfortable and anxious I felt about driving? I contemplated sharing my thirty reasons why I shouldn't be behind the wheel, but the weight of anger, fear, and humiliation held me back.

Gathering my composure, I made a decision. I asked the group to follow me as we headed toward the rental company to retrieve the van. We loaded our luggage into the spacious 15-passenger van, and one by one, we piled in. Meanwhile, the group continued to meet and greet each other, their cheerful mood contrasting sharply with my own inner turmoil.

As an introverted individual, I prefer to keep to myself, avoiding unnecessary interactions. The thought of spending an entire week with this group, whom I barely knew, filled me with apprehension. What would happen during our travels? Would I be able to handle it?

With a heavy heart, I adjusted the mirrors, fastened my seatbelt, and turned on the radio to create a semblance of normalcy. Trying to regain control of the situation, I asked for a volunteer to provide directions to the hotel. It seemed like a small task, but it allowed me to focus on something other than my own discomfort.

As I eased the van into reverse, an uneasy feeling settled in my gut. The sudden jolt as I hit the brakes made everyone lurch forward, and I could hear the shuffling of items sliding on the floor behind me. The awkwardness hung in the air like a heavy fog, and I couldn't shake the sensation that a million eyes were scrutinizing my every move.

The parking lot, once a sea of empty spaces, now felt like an audience witnessing my embarrassing spectacle. I couldn't help but berate myself internally, questioning how I had ended up with such a nerve-wracking assignment. Parked in the middle of the lot, the van seemed to symbolize my awkwardness and self-doubt.

Stepping out, I cautiously surveyed the surroundings, half-expecting to find evidence of my perceived collision. However, to my relief, there was nothing. I hadn't hit anything; it was all in my head. Yet, the weight of embarrassment lingered, and I couldn't shake the feeling of being a failure.

Behind the van, I took a moment to collect myself. The passengers, undoubtedly bewildered by my abrupt stop, awaited my next move. Gathering the shreds of my confidence, I re-entered the van and half-jokingly offered someone else the chance to take the wheel. Unanimously, they declined. One passenger, perhaps sensing my internal struggle, offered a nugget of encouragement, saying, "You'll get over this lack of confidence. Let's go."

Rolling my eyes and suppressing a frustrated sigh, I took deep breaths in an attempt to compose myself. With a reluctant determination, I put the van back in gear and awkwardly maneuvered it to a less conspicuous spot in the parking lot. The passengers, though probably puzzled by my erratic behavior, seemed eager to move on.

As I resumed driving, something peculiar happened. My vision shifted, and suddenly, everything became clear. It was as if a veil had been lifted, and I found myself perceiving the world in a new light. Operating the van felt different; it was as if I were piloting a low-flying plane. The once mundane task of driving now took on an exhilarating quality, and I couldn't help but marvel at the heightened awareness coursing through me.

As I stared at the daunting task ahead, the assignment seemed like an insurmountable mountain, casting its imposing shadow over my confidence. We were stranded at the airport, facing the challenge of getting from there to the hotel. My initial emotions were a cocktail of anger and pity, a bitter mix that wouldn't serve us well on this journey.

But dwelling on the negativity wasn't going to solve anything. I took a deep breath and decided to shift my thinking. Instead of succumbing to the belief that I couldn't handle it, I told myself, "I got this." It was a simple mantra, a declaration of my determination to overcome the obstacles that lay ahead.

As I embraced this newfound positive mindset, something remarkable happened. The task I once perceived as overwhelming now became an opportunity for me to prove my resilience. I focused on the details of the assignment, breaking it down into manageable steps. It was time to get from the airport to the hotel, and I was ready to take charge.

Recalling a familiar scripture, "I can do all things through Christ who strengthens me," I felt a surge of inspiration. It was like a double shot of espresso, providing the energy and confidence I needed to face the challenges head-on. With this newfound resolve, I approached the situation with a renewed sense of purpose.

Safe and sound, we arrived at the hotel. The journey had been a silent battle against the cacophony of negative thoughts that echoed in my mind. As I pulled up to the hotel entrance, a heavy scarf of bricks seemed to lift from my shoulders. The relief was palpable, but little did I know that my struggle was far from over.

In my haste to bring the van to a stop, I hit the brakes with a force that sent shockwaves through every passenger on board. The abrupt halt was met with a surprising eruption of applause. I sat there in disbelief, not accustomed to receiving praise for my driving skills. The passengers, seemingly unfazed by my lack of friendliness, congratulated me on conquering my fear and successfully navigating the van from one location to another.

However, as they exited the van with their luggage, a new wave of anxiety washed over me. I was left alone with my thoughts, grappling with the aftermath of my less-than-graceful entrance. The mask of shame hung heavy on my face, and questions swirled in my mind like a turbulent storm. What kind of first impression had I made? How would I recover from this professional unraveling? How could fear have such a powerful grip on my ability to execute a simple task?

Determined to regain my composure, I waited until everyone had disappeared into the hotel before taking a deep breath. The coast was clear, and I seized the opportunity to unwind and prepare my mind for the next challenge – parking the mammoth of a vehicle.

Shifting the gear from park to drive, I cautiously set off. My nerves were still on edge, and the weight of self-doubt clung to me like a shadow. As I approached the parking area, my focus intensified. The goal was clear: to park without a hitch and salvage whatever remained of my professional image.

Yet, just as I thought the worst was behind me, I miscalculated. The van careened into the curb, the left front tire flattening a once vibrant purple plant. It was a moment frozen in time, a snapshot of my failure etched into the landscape. I cringed at the sound of impact and glanced in the rearview mirrors, desperately searching for witnesses to my embarrassing blunder.

As I sat behind the wheel of the mammoth van, I couldn't help but feel overwhelmed by my own mischief. I had attempted to park the van earlier, but my negative thinking had taken over, leaving me frustrated and defeated. However, I knew I couldn't just leave the van parked haphazardly, so I decided to give it another try.

With determination in my heart, I started to maneuver the van around corners, trying to find the perfect parking spot. After 15 minutes of backing up and repositioning myself, I finally managed to squeeze into a parking spot, but only by a quarter. I felt a sense of accomplishment, but it was short-lived as I realized I still couldn't fully park the van.

In that moment, I found myself sinking into a circle of defeat, misery, and frustration. I questioned why this task seemed so difficult for me. Negative thoughts flooded my mind, and I began to doubt my driving skills. I felt like giving up, ready to sit and mope in my own self-pity.

But then, a realization hit me like a bolt of lightning. Why was I trying to park near other vehicles? It seemed so obvious now. I looked around and spotted a spot far away from the cluster of cars where I could park as crooked as my ability permitted. It wasn't ideal, but it was a solution that worked for me at that moment.

The next day marked the beginning of our training. We had all received our agendas beforehand, so we knew when we needed to leave the hotel to arrive at the training facility on time. Determined to start the day on a positive note, I made sure to rest and meditate on a biblical principle that would shift my mindset into a better place.

I felt refreshed and ready to conquer the day ahead when I woke up. I had the van waiting, ready to transport the passengers. As we set off toward the training facility, I couldn't help but feel a surge of nervousness. The route involved driving on the expressway, something that always made me anxious.

However, I refused to let my fear control me. I kept reminding myself that I had the skills to handle this mammoth van on the expressway. I repeated positive affirmations in my mind, convincing myself that I could do it.

As we merged onto the expressway, I felt a mix of apprehension and determination. Surprisingly, our commute was relatively smooth. The van moved steadily, and my internal uneasiness started to fade away. I was proud of myself for facing my fear head-on and overcoming it, even if it was just a small victory.

As we approached the exit we needed to take, my heart started racing with anticipation. I knew I had to change lanes, but just as I was about to make the move, a tractor-trailer swerved toward us. Panic washed over me, and in that moment of fear, I instinctively whipped the steering wheel to the side, trying to avoid a collision.

The van lurched abruptly, and before I knew it, we were on the side of the expressway, dangerously close to tipping over into a ditch. Shock consumed me, and it felt as though the air had been sucked out of the van. My heart pounded in my chest as if I had just finished running a 5K race.

Once I regained a semblance of composure, I looked around to check on my passengers. They appeared disoriented, their faces reflecting the impact of the sudden maneuver. I asked if everyone was okay, and thankfully, no injuries were reported. I apologized for the abrupt pullover, assuring them that I had done the best I could at that moment.

One of the passengers, seemingly the most composed among them, began picking up the items that had flown around during the sudden stop. They encouraged me to regain my courage and continue our journey. Their words resonated with me, and I made a firm decision not to surrender to this challenging moment.

Taking a deep breath, I steered the van back onto the road, determined to push forward. I refused to let this incident define my abilities as a driver. With each passing mile, my confidence grew, and I focused on the road ahead, determined to get us safely to our destination.

Over the course of the week, as I transported my classmates to and from class, dinners, and sightseeing adventures, I began to evolve into a professional mammoth van chauffeur. Each day presented new obstacles and challenges, but what truly mattered was how I responded to them.

Instead of allowing myself to be consumed by negative emotions, I chose to arrest those thoughts and dismiss them. I realized that dwelling on the negative mindset would not yield any positive results. Instead, I shifted my focus to positive thoughts and phrases that encouraged me to think outside the box.

Every time I accidentally hit a curb while maneuvering the van, I acknowledged the mistake but refused to dwell on it. I understood that mistakes were a part of the learning process, and what truly mattered was my ability to adapt and improve. With each passing day, my driving skills improved, and I became more comfortable behind the wheel of the mammoth van.

By the end of the driving journey, I had mastered the art of parking the van in any spot. What once seemed like an insurmountable task now felt like second nature to me. I merged on and off the expressways with ease, as if I were driving a small Ford Focus. My ability to navigate through traffic had strengthened, all because I had chosen to embrace the challenges rather than succumb to them.

Reflecting on the entire experience, I realized that it was not just about driving skills. It was about mindset and resilience. I had learned that success often comes from our ability to respond positively to interference and obstacles. Instead of dwelling on the "why me" mentality, I focused on finding solutions and pushing forward.

As I dropped off my coworkers at the training facility, I couldn't help but feel a sense of pride and accomplishment. We had arrived safely despite the challenges we had faced along the way. I had transformed from a hesitant driver into a confident one, ready to take on any obstacle that came my way.

This driving journey has taught me valuable life lessons. It has shown me the power of a positive mindset, the importance of perseverance, and the rewards that come from embracing challenges head-on. As I parked the mammoth van one last time,

I couldn't help but smile. I had not only conquered the physical act of driving, but I had also conquered my own doubts and fears.

This experience would forever serve as a reminder that with determination and the right mindset, anything is possible. I had chosen to succeed, and in doing so, I had unlocked my true potential as a driver and as an individual.

I've always believed that life presents us with opportunities in unexpected forms. Sometimes, these opportunities disguise themselves as inconveniences or hardships. It's all about perspective. Instead of viewing unfamiliar tasks as obstacles, I choose to see them as chances to birth a better version of myself. This mindset shift has been my guiding light, leading me to embrace challenges with open arms and a determination to grow.

One key takeaway I've learned is to approach challenging assignments as a pathway to acquiring new skills. Each task, no matter how daunting, comes with a unique set of lessons. When faced with a new challenge, I take a moment to reflect: What skill can I gain from this experience? What steps do I need to take to accomplish the task at hand? These questions serve as a roadmap for my personal development journey.

Accepting challenging assignments is like stepping into a learning loop. It's an opportunity to stretch my capabilities, broaden my horizons, and create room for growth. Every time I push myself beyond my comfort zone, I enter a cycle of continuous learning. It's not just about completing the task; it's about the transformation that occurs during the process.

One action step I consistently take is to believe in myself. Being my own cheerleader has been a game-changer. While external support is valuable, there won't always be a group of supporters to push you forward. I was fortunate to have encountered strangers who encouraged me when I doubted myself, but I also realized the importance of self-empowerment. Knowing how to lift yourself up and change your course when needed is a skill that pays dividends in the journey of personal growth.

As I navigate through these challenges, I often recall the wise words of Abraham Maslow: "In any given moment, we have two options: to step forward into growth or to step back into safety." These words resonate with the essence of my journey – choosing growth over the safety of the familiar. It's a conscious decision to face the unknown, armed with the belief that every step forward contributes to my evolution.

Dwayne Johnson's quote serves as a constant reminder that success is a gradual process. "Success isn't overnight. It's when every day you get a little better than the day before. It all adds up." This perspective helps me stay focused on the incremental progress I make. Each day is an opportunity to improve, learn, and accumulate small victories that collectively shape the path to success.

In practical terms, this philosophy translates into taking on stretch assignments. I intentionally seek tasks that are unfamiliar to me, challenging my existing skill set. It's a deliberate effort to move beyond the comfort of what I already know and venture into the realms of the unknown. With each new assignment, I find myself facing uncertainties, but it's within these uncertainties that I discover my true potential.

Chapter 7: Discovering Courage

"Your mindset is the compass that guides your actions and decisions. Change your mindset, and you change your direction."

-Unknown

Stressful situations often test our resilience and focus. When faced with these challenges, I've learned to concentrate on the task at hand and silence any self-doubt. Instead of letting uncertainty creep in, I remind myself that I am capable and can overcome whatever comes my way. This mindset has been instrumental in navigating various trials, including a memorable experience during my travels from Baltimore, MD, to different parts of Virginia.

I remember those early mornings vividly. The alarm would ring at 3 a.m., pulling me out of the comfort of my bed. As I packed my things and stepped out into the quiet streets of Baltimore, the weight of the long day ahead loomed over me. My job required me to visit multiple locations within my territory in Virginia, a task that demanded early starts and extensive travel.

Driving through the dark, empty roads, I sought solace in music. Music has always been a significant part of my life, especially Black Gospel music. The powerful voices and uplifting messages provided a spiritual connection that I cherished deeply. However, as I crossed into more remote areas, the radio stations that played my preferred music became scarce. The absence of Black Gospel music left a void that needed to be filled.

At first, I felt a sense of frustration. The familiar tunes that usually set the tone for my day were replaced by static or unfamiliar genres. Some of my favorite gospel artists are Kirk Franklin, Fred Hammond, Yolanda Adams, Marvin Sapp, Tamela Mann and the list goes on. I tried switching to nonspiritual music, but it didn't resonate with me in the same way. It was in these moments of limited options that I stumbled upon Christian music, a genre I had previously overlooked.

Artists like Casting Crowns, Chris Tomlin, MercyMe, and Jeremy Camp began to fill the silence in my car. Initially, I was hesitant and critical. The music was different from what I was accustomed to, and I struggled to connect with it. But as the miles rolled on and the songs continued to play, something unexpected happened. The lyrics and melodies began to grow on me. I started to listen more intently to the words, understanding the messages of hope, faith, and love embedded within them.

This new genre of music became more than just a background noise. It transformed my long car rides into moments of reflection and spiritual growth. The songs helped me strengthen my connection with God in a way I hadn't experienced before. Each artist brought something unique to the table, and their music began to speak to me on a deeper level. The once dreaded drives became a time of peace and preparation, setting the tone for my interactions throughout the day.

As I listened to the music, I found myself reassured by the messages of perseverance and trust in God's plan. The lyrics reminded me to stay focused and keep faith, even when the road ahead seemed uncertain. This shift in perspective was crucial. Instead of viewing the long hours on the road as a burden, I began to see them as an opportunity for personal growth and spiritual nourishment.

My morning drives set the stage for a positive mindset. The peaceful tunes and uplifting messages prepared me to face the day with a calm and focused demeanor. I arrived at my destinations with a sense of inner peace, ready to engage with anyone I encountered. This positive energy was infectious, making my interactions more meaningful and productive.

After a long day's work, the drive back home became a time of decompression. The music helped me unwind, letting go of any stress or tension from the day. By the time I pulled into my driveway, I was in a state of calm, ready to spend quality time with my family. This routine of using music to manage my mindset turned a potentially negative situation into a rewarding experience.

As I look back on my professional journey, I've come to realize that the way we think can profoundly influence our outcomes. This insight didn't come to me easily, but rather through a series of challenging experiences that tested my resilience and forced me to rethink how I approached both my work and personal life.

Let me take you through one of the pivotal moments in my career, which involved relocating from Baltimore, MD, to the bustling market of New York City. This story isn't just about a move; it's about adapting, balancing priorities, and leveraging mindset to turn a daunting situation into a success story.

I was on a special assignment on the West Coast, working tirelessly and emotionally taxed from delivering difficult news to hundreds of employees. During this already stressful time, I received the shocking news that my territory was being dissolved. I had 60 days to find another job. This news hit me hard. I had a meltdown. I wasn't financially prepared to take a pause in my career, and the future seemed uncertain.

But life has a way of presenting opportunities disguised as challenges. Soon after, I was offered a lateral move to the New York market. At first glance, it didn't seem like an ideal solution. I had a husband who was well-rooted in his career in Maryland and three school-aged children. The thought of relocating brought back memories of my own childhood, where I attended around 13 different public schools due to frequent moves. The idea was far from appealing.

After assessing our financial health and weighing all possible options, my husband and I decided that relocating to New York was the best path forward. It wasn't just about my career; it was about making a decision that would benefit our entire family.

I knew this move would be challenging, but I also saw it as an opportunity to change our lives for the better. This mindset shift—from viewing the move as a burden to seeing it as an opportunity—was crucial.

The move turned out to be a blessing in disguise. We purchased a beautiful five-bedroom home on a couple of acres. My husband landed an incredible job with the State of New York, and our son thrived, wrestling competitively throughout the state.

We embraced everything New York had to offer: Times Square, Niagara Falls, Long Island Beaches, and more. These experiences enriched our lives in ways we hadn't anticipated, creating lasting memories and strengthening our family bond.

Professionally, the move to New York City opened doors I hadn't imagined. The high visibility of the market brought numerous opportunities for growth and exposure. I led the HR department, a role that came with significant responsibilities and visibility. Dignitaries visited frequently, and I attended elite, invite-only conferences. These experiences not only enhanced my professional skills but also expanded my network, proving invaluable in my career progression.

However, this success didn't come without its challenges. Balancing work and personal life were crucial. I had to manage long hours and travel demands, ensuring I didn't overextend myself. One particular instance stands out: After a 12-hour workday that started at 7 AM, I faced a three-hour drive that, due to road conditions, turned into four. This experience taught me the importance of factoring in travel time and the need to balance all priorities—work, travel, and personal well-being.

Planning your routes in advance and understanding the required travel paths is critical for anyone who frequently finds themselves on the road. This lesson hit home for me during a recent trip, and looking back, it would have been much wiser to stay in West Virginia and travel in the morning. But hindsight is always 20/20, isn't it?

I was on a business trip touring one of my sites in West Virginia. As usual, I engaged in conversations with my associates about various local recommendations—places to stay, restaurants to try, and so on. During one such chat, a group of associates kept asking about my departure time. Curious, I finally asked them why it mattered. They expressed concern about my travel plans, particularly if I intended to drive far away at night.

Their worry piqued my interest, so I pressed for more details. They warned me about cannibals in the mountains and the dangers for "outsiders" who might stop in that area, especially after dark. They mentioned people going missing or encountering bizarre and unsafe situations in the mountainous region. I had to drive through these mountains from Beckley, WV, to Danville, VA—a trip that I was about to undertake with my business partner. We were in separate cars, but both of us were now anxious to leave before nightfall.

Unfortunately, work kept us busy, and we couldn't leave the facility until around 7 PM. The drive to our next destination, our hotel, was approximately three hours. As soon as we started, it became clear how treacherous the journey would be. The mountains were pitch black, with no highway or streetlights, only the occasional dim light from houses far off in the distance. Heavy fog enveloped us, and the narrow, two-lane roads were filled with sharp turns and steep elevations. One miscalculation could send us over a deadly cliff, and the flimsy wire barriers did little to reassure us.

At one point, I almost collided with a speeding tractor-trailer as it barreled around a sharp curve. The journey felt like an endless, nerve-wracking ascent and descent through a never-ending spiral. I stayed as close as possible to my business partner's car, relying on her tail lights for guidance and a sense of safety. My thoughts were consumed with fears of breaking down or getting into an accident and being stranded in this desolate area. The rumors of cannibals kept creeping back into my mind, amplifying my anxiety. I prayed continuously, hoping to make it through this hazardous stretch of road alive.

There was no turning back; we were too far gone, and there were no signs of nearby towns or chain hotels to provide refuge. When we finally exited the mountainous region, the relief was immense. We found ourselves on a normal, flat road and quickly decided to stop at Buffalo Wild Wings to grab some food to go. The simple act of picking up our order felt like a celebration.

Reaching the Hampton Inn never felt so satisfying. The ordeal left both my business partner and me physically and mentally drained. We both vowed never to travel that route from Beckley to Danville again, especially not at night. She echoed my fears and shared the same sense of relief at having made it through unscathed.

This experience taught me a valuable lesson about preparation and the importance of avoiding unnecessary risks. Planning your travel routes carefully can prevent a lot of unnecessary stress and potential danger. My associates' warnings, although seemingly based on local folklore and rumors, served as a crucial reminder of the importance of local knowledge. While the tales of cannibalism and inbreeding might have been exaggerated, the real danger lay in the treacherous driving conditions of the Blue Ridge Mountains at night.

The Blue Ridge Mountains are stunningly beautiful, and the drive during the day offers breathtaking scenery. However, this experience has made it clear that certain routes are best navigated in daylight. The mountains can be a wonderful sight, but they also hold real dangers that are often overshadowed by local legends and gossip.

I plan my travels more meticulously, ensuring I understand the routes and the best times to travel. This experience also highlighted the importance of listening to local advice and taking it seriously, even if it sounds like mere folklore. The mountains, while beautiful, demand respect and caution, especially for those unfamiliar with the terrain.

Always prioritize safety and plan your travels to avoid unnecessary risks. The beauty of the journey should not be overshadowed by fear and danger. By planning ahead, you can enjoy the sights without compromising your safety. This lesson, learned the hard way, will stay with me, reminding me always to respect the journey and the path ahead.

Changing Your Outcome through Mindset

Reflecting on this journey, I realized that changing your outcome starts with changing your mindset. Here are some tips that can help you:

1. **Embrace Change**: View changes as opportunities rather than obstacles. This shift in perspective can open up new paths and possibilities.

2. **Balance Priorities**: Ensure that you balance work, travel, and personal life. Overextending yourself can lead to burnout and decreased productivity.

3. **Plan Ahead**: Factor in all elements of your workday, including travel and potential delays, to avoid unnecessary stress.

4. Stay Positive: Maintain a positive attitude, even in challenging situations. Positivity can significantly impact your ability to navigate difficulties.

5. Seek Support: Don't hesitate to lean on your support network, whether it's family, friends, or colleagues. They can provide valuable perspectives and help you through tough times.

Chapter 8: You Got This!

"Transforming from victim to victor is an empowering journey, revealing the true strength within when you see the complete picture."

-Jennifer Logan

I was out of town for a business meeting when I got the call. My childcare provider, Karen, was on the other end, her voice shaking. She told me a police officer had charged her with neglect, specifically neglect of my children. I felt a knot form in my stomach as she explained. She had returned a shopping cart to the cart corral, and when she got back to the car, a police officer was waiting. He claimed she had neglected my infant daughter, Kya, by leaving her in the car while she returned the cart. Karen sounded desperate, fearing she could lose her daycare license and business.

Immediately, I asked my husband to get our children and not return them to Karen's care until we had more information. I knew I had to address this situation personally, so I requested to leave work and head home.

When I finally spoke with the officer, his version of events was starkly different. A good Samaritan had noticed Kya left alone in the car. They had waited for someone to appear but saw no one nearby. After about 20 minutes, they called the police. The officer said he witnessed Karen leaving the grocery store with a heaping cart full of groceries. She had left Kya in the car the entire time she was shopping during the winter. I was furious. This wasn't a quick return of a shopping cart; she had left my infant alone for an extended period during extremely cold conditions.

I needed more context, so I talked to my son about Ms. Karen. His response was tepid. "She's okay," he said when I asked what he thought of her. I probed further, asking if she took good care of him and his sisters. "Yes, most of the time," he replied. When I asked when she didn't take good care of them, he mentioned only one instance: When she cooked food with cheese, knowing he didn't like it. Otherwise, he didn't have any complaints.

Despite my son's generally positive feedback, I couldn't get past the fact that Karen had left Kya alone in the car. It was an unforgivable lapse in judgment. The officer's account left no room for doubt—Karen had endangered my daughter's safety.

Karen had asked me to write a letter vouching for her, but how could I? Trust was the foundation of any caregiving relationship, and she had shattered it. If the charges were true, she didn't deserve to have children in her care. The idea that my daughter could have been harmed was too much to bear. My primary responsibility was to protect my children, and leaving them in the care of someone so negligent was out of the question.

One day, we went shopping at the local mall. I parked in the Macy's parking lot, and my son immediately mentioned, "This is Ms. Karen's favorite store." Intrigued, I asked him how he knew this. He replied that she parks the car near this store and disappears for hours. I felt a knot in my stomach and asked if he ever went inside with her. He said no. She left him and his sisters in the car while she shopped. My heart sank.

My son explained that she would tell him he was in charge, leaving sticky notes with times on them. When the car clock matched the time on the note, he had to feed the infant her bottle. She had even taught him how to mix a bottle with water and powdered formula. He described it so clearly: the exact time he should give the bottle and the ratio of water to formula. I couldn't believe what I was hearing. My children were left in a car, under the supervision of my 8-year-old son, Alec, to care for his 4-year-old sister, Jayla, and their 8-week-old baby sister, Kya. I had entrusted their care to a licensed childcare provider.

The betrayal was immense. I trusted her completely with my children's lives. She called me repeatedly, begging me to write a letter to her attorney to help her resume providing childcare services and get the charges dropped. She insisted that since my children were involved, my support would make all the difference. It took every ounce of strength to finally call her back. I needed to compose myself first because I was overwhelmed with anger, hurt, and a sense of deep betrayal.

When I spoke to her, I was blunt. I told her I would not be writing any letters. I expressed my hope that she would be held accountable for her actions, even imprisoned, for how she had treated my children. She had betrayed my trust and jeopardized the well-being and safety of my kids. She did not deserve to be in any business involving children. Forgiveness seemed impossible at that moment. The hardest part was dealing with the urge to hold onto my anger.

I remembered a quote I once heard: "Unforgiveness is like drinking poison and expecting someone else to suffer from what you consumed." It resonated deeply with me. Holding onto the anger and pain wasn't hurting her; it was hurting me. Most often, those who hurt us forget what they did while we continue to relive the pain. My children are my heart and soul. Their well-being is my priority, and I work so hard to provide for them. Knowing they were under the care of such a reckless woman brought up so many unsettling emotions. I could feel the anger consuming me.

Living in the same community, I feared how I would react if I saw her out and about. I needed to pray and ask God to help me with forgiveness. I didn't want to seek physical revenge, though I felt an overwhelming urge to confront her for neglecting my kids. But I realized this wasn't my fight. I needed to give it to God.

I came across a biblical verse that guided me: "In Romans 12:17-21, Paul explains that Christians must be ready to forgive everyone, not just other Christians. We should never return evil for evil. As far as we can, we should live in peace with everyone. Furthermore, it's never okay to seek revenge when people wrong us, even if those people are really evil." Standing on God's word, I learned to trust Him. I decided to forgive Karen, not for her sake, but for mine. I couldn't afford to let hatred fester and consume me.

When I told Karen I forgave her, it was a moment of release for me. I made it clear that forgiveness did not mean she would escape accountability. I informed her that I would see her in court, where she would be held responsible for her actions.

My children's well-being was paramount. They needed to know that I stood up for them and that their safety was non-negotiable. This experience taught me a lot about trust, betrayal, and forgiveness. It reinforced the importance of following my instincts and the necessity of thorough vetting when it comes to the care of my children. This chapter in our lives was painful, but it was also a lesson in resilience and faith.

At court, her lawyer approached my husband and me, asking if I would consider speaking on her behalf to request leniency in her punishment. Without hesitation, I firmly said, "No." He attempted to offer an explanation, but I politely reiterated my refusal and told him to walk away before demanding reimbursement for every dime I paid her as a licensed childcare provider. Looking genuinely remorseful, her husband apologized sincerely for his wife's actions. After that, they both walked away.

Her daycare license was revoked, and she faced charges of neglect. Although my initial reaction was to want her jailed, she didn't end up behind bars. This was her first offense, and she was shown grace. I had to let the situation go, even though it was difficult. With no immediate childcare available, I turned to my mother-in-law, who graciously agreed to take care of my three children for the summer. This arrangement allowed us to continue working while searching for a new daycare provider.

During this trying time, I cried every day. The absence of my kids was a constant ache. They were my source of peace after a long day at work, and knowing they were safe with my mother-in-law didn't entirely ease the heartache of missing them. The bond I shared with my children was my anchor, and being apart from them felt like a part of me was missing.

Pointers on Forgiveness:

1. Acknowledge Your Emotions: It's crucial to accept and understand your feelings of hurt and anger. Recognize that these emotions are valid and part of the healing process.

2. Empathy and Understanding: Try to understand the situation from the other person's perspective. This doesn't mean excusing their actions but recognizing their humanity and possible reasons behind their behavior.

3. Letting Go for Your Peace: Holding onto resentment and anger can be more damaging to you than to the person who wronged you. Forgiveness is about freeing yourself from the burden of these negative emotions and finding peace.

In the end, forgiveness was a gift I gave myself. It was about reclaiming my peace and allowing myself to heal. It was about understanding that while the past cannot be changed, the future holds endless possibilities for growth and happiness.

Forgiveness taught me resilience and the importance of letting go. It reminded me of the strength within me and the power of moving forward with a lighter heart. And most importantly, it reaffirmed the unbreakable bond with my children, a bond that no circumstance could ever diminish.

Chapter 9: Making A Connection

"Opportunities can look as a daunting obstacle or a chance to magnify your brilliance."

-Jennifer Logan

When I was asked to host a Women's Leadership Conference in Upstate New York, I felt a mix of excitement and apprehension. Living four hours away from the city where the event was to be held, I had never been to that part of New York before. To make matters more challenging, this wasn't a role I volunteered for; I was voluntold, meaning I was nominated and accepted because I was needed. Hosting a major event for the #1 retailer in the world in unfamiliar territory was very intimidating and exciting at the same time.

The conference was set to include primarily women from across the Midwest and East Coast, with a few men joining as well. There was no blueprint for this event. I had to gather ideas from other events and stakeholders who approved the event. My responsibilities included securing a venue, managing reservations for out-of-town guests, finding speakers, sending invitations, managing the attendee list, recruiting the event planning team, outlining conference content, and, unexpectedly, stepping in as the MC at the last minute when the scheduled person was unable to make it.

The role of a host encompassed numerous tasks, each critical to the event's success. Securing a venue that could accommodate all attendees was the first step. I had to find a location that was accessible, comfortable, and suitable for our needs. Managing reservations for out-of-town guests was another significant responsibility. Ensuring that everyone had a place to stay and that all accommodations were satisfactory required meticulous planning and coordination.

Finding speakers was both a challenging and rewarding task. I reached out to various professionals who could inspire and educate our attendees. Sending invitations and managing the attendee list was another crucial aspect. I had to make sure that everyone received their invitations on time and that our list was up-to-date.

Recruiting the event planning team was essential. I needed to trust each person to deliver on their assignments. Delegation became a valuable lesson. I had to rely on my team, knowing that I couldn't do everything myself. Outlining the conference content involved careful planning to ensure that every segment was relevant and engaging.

As the event approached, everything seemed to be falling into place. Then, at the last minute, our MC was unavailable. Suddenly, I found myself stepping into the role. I had never MC'd an event before and didn't have time to stress about it. I just had to step up and get the job done. Given my deep involvement in planning, I was probably the best person for the job. I knew the agenda inside out and had merged all the presentations from the speakers.

(The link to the video of the class prank

https://m.facebook.com/story.php?story_fbid=1188118027875030&id=100000305335120)

The first day of the conference arrived, and I felt a mix of nerves and excitement. As the MC, my role was to introduce the speakers, keep the agenda on track, recap after every segment, and engage the audience. Despite my initial apprehension, I quickly found my rhythm. Introducing the speakers and getting them on stage felt natural. I made sure to recap after every segment, highlighting key points and encouraging the audience to reflect on what they had learned.

One of the most rewarding aspects was seeing the audience's reactions. There was a lot of laughter, applause, and smiles throughout the conference. The energy in the room was palpable. I received numerous compliments and accolades for my role as an MC. Many attendees stated that I was a natural at moving the crowd and keeping them engaged. Knowing I had done a good job was incredibly fulfilling.

The two-day conference was filled with valuable insights and inspiring moments. The panelists and presenters did an amazing job. They shared their knowledge and experiences, empowering the audience to level up in their careers. The feedback from attendees was overwhelmingly positive. They walked away feeling empowered and fired up to use the information they had gained to better their careers.

I've always prided myself on having a "can do" mindset. This mindset has often led me to take on tasks outside my comfort zone, and it's how I found myself preparing for a daunting yet exhilarating stretch assignment as a master of ceremonies (MC) at a significant conference. With my reputation on the line, the stakes were high. However, when I finally arrived on site and saw everything come to fruition, I felt an overwhelming sense of accomplishment. Once again, I had conquered a challenging assignment.

Planning a conference is no small feat. It requires meticulous attention to detail, seamless coordination, and the ability to anticipate and mitigate potential issues. Throughout this process, I held several COE (correction of error) meetings. These meetings were crucial for identifying areas for improvement and ensuring future events would run even smoother. Continuous learning and adaptation are vital in event planning, and these meetings provided invaluable insights.

My journey took another significant turn when I was selected to become a Leadership Essentials trainer for Walmart Stores Inc. The certification process was intense, involving rigorous training sessions and evaluations. Each session required four trainers, and it was a four-day marathon of facilitation, group activities, and capstones. The pressure was immense, but the sense of responsibility and opportunity for impact kept me motivated.

The deadline to train our entire Division loomed large, and I was tasked with leading "The Last Call" training session of the year in Lynchburg, VA. This session was particularly challenging because it was designed for four facilitators, yet I was to lead it solo. The weight of this responsibility was palpable, and sleep became a luxury as I prepared tirelessly for the four days of content delivery.

The venue in Lynchburg, VA, was a familiar one. I had held many meetings at this hotel and had developed a great rapport with the sales manager. This familiarity provided a small comfort amidst the whirlwind of preparation. Despite the exhaustion, the class was a resounding success. Participants from various regions attended, each eager to gain their Leadership Essentials certification. My goal was to make the sessions engaging, fun, and impactful, and I'm proud to say I achieved that. The participants left with a renewed vigor and spark to excel in their roles.

However, the learning wasn't one-sided. The participants taught me invaluable lessons about balance and the importance of taking care of oneself. They observed my relentless preparation schedule—arriving early in the morning and staying late into the evening to set up for the next day and clean up after each session. Initially, I declined their offers to help, wanting to protect their experience from any extra work. But their persistence paid off. They urged me to explore the town and enjoy some downtime. Reluctantly, I agreed.

On the third night, the class organized a team activity: summer mountain tubing. It was an unforgettable experience. We laughed, screamed, and bonded in ways that transcended the classroom setting. This team activity was the most fun I'd had in a long time, and it was a powerful reminder that those we lead or work with appreciate seeing us enjoy life and let loose occasionally.

The final day of class dawned with the promise of wrapping up our capstone project. I walked into the meeting room, expecting to see my students eager and ready for the presentations. Instead, I was greeted with a scene I could never have anticipated. The entire room was filled with pillows, each one adorned with a makeshift face drawn on a paper plate. Some pillows sported scarves, hats, shirts, or even pieces of jewelry. It took me a moment to register what was happening. Every seat was filled, but not by my students—by these pillow people.

I stood there, slack-jawed, taking in the creativity and the sheer effort that had gone into the prank. There was an absurdity to it but also a sense of camaraderie. My students had managed to find time in their busy schedules to pull off something so elaborate. And the fact that no one was actually in class at 8 am, as required, only added to the hilarity. I could hardly believe it.

After a moment, I snapped out of my stupor and did the only logical thing—I recorded a video. I wanted to capture this moment, to have a record of their ingenuity and the bond we had formed over the course of the class. As I walked around the room, filming the pillows in their various outfits, I couldn't help but laugh. It was a testament to how comfortable they had become with me and each other, to the point where they felt they could pull off such a prank.

As I panned the camera across the room, I noticed something else that made me chuckle—the hotel staff had joined in on the fun. They had supplied additional pillows from empty rooms, adding to the overall effect. It was a small detail, but it meant a lot. It showed that our group had made an impression on more than just ourselves. We had created a ripple effect of joy and mischief that had spread to others.

When my students finally started trickling in, their grins were wide, and their laughter infectious. We spent the first part of our session reminiscing about the past few days, sharing stories and inside jokes. We had started as a group of strangers, but we had become well acquainted and created great memories together.

This prank was the culmination of all the trust and rapport we had built.

As the laughter died down, I realized there was a lesson to be learned here beyond the professional curriculum. My participants had taught me to have fun at work. The experience reminded me that life is too short not to relax and enjoy every minute. It's important to find joy intentionally, even in professional settings. The ability to laugh, to take a moment to breathe, and to enjoy the company of others is invaluable.

So, the final day of class wasn't just about presenting projects and wrapping up coursework. It was about celebrating the journey we had taken together, the bond we had formed, and the joy we had found in each other's company. It was a day that reinforced a simple yet profound truth: life is too short not to enjoy every minute and intentionally seek out joy, even at work.

Chapter 10: Believe in Your Ability to Succeed

"Amazing things happen internally and externally when you confidently use your seat at the table."

-Jennifer Logan

Having a seat at the table isn't about the physical act of pulling up a chair and sitting down. It's about being present, involved, and having your voice heard in conversations and decision-making processes. I learned this lesson firsthand during a roundtable discussion with an executive team on the topics of diversity and inclusion. I had valuable insights to share, but two other participants dominated the conversation, leaving my thoughts unheard. Here's what I learned from that experience.

1. Don't Assume You'll Be Given a Chance to Speak

At first, I sat there, waiting for the perfect moment to jump in and share my reflections. I thought that, eventually, room would be made for me to naturally join the conversation. This timid approach was a mistake. By simply waiting for an opportunity, I allowed myself to be viewed as shy and lacking assertiveness. From this experience, I developed a strategy to assert myself and ensure my voice is heard.

2. Your Voice is Valuable

Eventually, I mustered the courage to speak up. When I did, I realized a crucial lesson: what I have to say matters. My opinions are important and can drive positive change. This realization is vital for anyone. Recognizing and respecting the value of your voice is the first step in making meaningful contributions.

3. Your Lack of Participation Will Allow Chances to Slip Away

This discussion with senior leadership was a rare opportunity to be heard. I nearly missed it because I wasn't assertive enough. To strengthen your executive presence, it's essential to participate fully when opportunities arise. Passive participation isn't enough; you must actively engage to make an impact.

4. We Are Not Born Effective Communicators

Effective communication takes practice and training. It's natural to feel uneasy about being vocal at first. Remember, we are all shaped by our experiences and lessons. If you feel you've failed in a moment, use that experience as motivation to improve. Communication skills develop over time with continuous effort and reflection.

5. There Is Always Room to Grow

Even as a leadership development professional, I have had moments where I felt ineffective and unheard. This experience reminded me that there's always room for growth. Believing that you've reached a point where you can no longer learn and improve is a mistake. Embrace every opportunity to enhance your communication skills.

Reflecting on this experience, I developed a refined approach to ensure my voice is heard in future discussions.

Here's what worked for me:

a. Preparation Is Key

Before the meeting, I thoroughly prepared my thoughts and ideas. Having a clear understanding of what I wanted to say boosted my confidence. I also anticipated possible counterarguments and thought about how to address them. Preparation helped me feel more in control and ready to contribute meaningfully.

b. Find the Right Moment

In a dynamic conversation, waiting for a perfect moment might mean missing out entirely. Instead, I learned to create opportunities. I looked for natural pauses or transitions in the discussion to insert my points. It's about being proactive rather than reactive.

c. Be Concise and Clear

When I finally spoke, I ensured my points were concise and clear. Rambling can dilute your message and lose the audience's attention. By being direct and to the point, I made my contributions more impactful.

d. Use Body Language

Non-verbal cues play a significant role in communication. I used confident body language to signal my readiness to speak. Maintaining eye contact, sitting up straight, and leaning slightly forward showed I was engaged and prepared to contribute.

e. Follow Up

After the meeting, I followed up with key participants to reiterate my points and discuss them further. This not only reinforced my contributions but also demonstrated my commitment to the topic.

f. Seek Feedback

To improve, I sought feedback from colleagues and mentors. Constructive criticism helped me identify areas for improvement and refine my approach. Continuous learning and adaptation are crucial for becoming a more effective communicator.

g. Practice Assertiveness

Assertiveness is a skill that can be developed with practice. I practiced speaking up in smaller, less intimidating settings to build my confidence. Gradually, this made it easier to assert myself in more challenging environments.

h. Stay Composed Under Pressure

It's easy to feel overwhelmed in high-stakes discussions. I focused on staying composed and not letting nerves get the better of me. Deep breathing and positive self-talk helped me maintain my calm and clarity.

i. Believe in Yourself

Ultimately, confidence in your abilities is crucial. Believing that your voice matters and your contributions are valuable is the foundation for effective participation. This self-assurance will come across in your communication and enhance your presence at the table.

Having a seat at the table is about more than just being physically present. It's about actively participating, asserting yourself, and ensuring your voice is heard. My experience taught me valuable lessons about the importance of preparation, assertiveness, and continuous growth. By embracing these principles, anyone can become a more effective and confident communicator. Remember, your voice is valuable; with the right approach, you can make a meaningful impact in any discussion.

The day the Vice President visited our territory started like any other travel day. We arrived at our destination in the evening, and our market manager had arranged dinner at an Indian restaurant. We agreed to meet in the lobby at a specific time. As luck would have it, when I got on the elevator, the VP and other high-ranking corporate officials were already inside. There were three men and myself, all from our Fortune 50 company. The elevator ride that should have been routine quickly turned into a nightmare.

The elevator stopped abruptly, and an alarm sounded. We were stuck between floors, and panic set in. I've never been fond of close quarters, and being trapped in an elevator only added to my anxiety. The hotel called the fire department, and the emergency response team contacted us through the elevator emergency phone. They asked if we were okay. Outside of being nervous about the company I was in and being stuck in the elevator without knowing what had happened, the main question on my mind was how we were going to get out safely.

The emergency response team asked who needed help and who had pressed the emergency call button. The four of us looked at each other, completely baffled. The VP raised his hands and said, "Not me." The other VPs did the same. I raised both of my hands and said, "I didn't do it." With my hands raised high, I noticed everyone was looking at me with slight chuckles. I realized my buttocks were firmly pressed against the emergency alert button. It was embarrassing.

The emergency personnel forced the elevator down to the main lobby level. Awaiting our arrival was my entire market team, roughly seven of my peers, along with a host of emergency personnel. If I could have disappeared at that moment, I would have. It was mortifying. What a way to make a first impression.

We eventually made it to dinner. I rode with my Regional Manager and Divisional Vice President. I was impressed with the Divisional VP's gentlemanly behavior; he insisted I sit in the front seat and even opened and closed the door for me. The Market Manager drove us to the restaurant. I appreciated that they didn't mention the elevator fiasco during the ride.

When we arrived at the restaurant, we met the rest of our party. As soon as we approached our table, my company VP announced that the seat next to him was reserved for me. People had to get up and move so I could sit to his right. If I could have shrunk, I would have. My company VP fixed me an appetizer plate and handed it to me. I'm a finicky eater, so I had to muster up the courage and taste bud tolerance to explore the plate he prepared. This was a very unique and rewarding experience, considering I'm a cautious eater.

As we settled in, Nacho proceeded to tell the party what had happened in the elevator. My teammates looked at me in disbelief and shared my embarrassment. While the experience was traumatizing at the time, in hindsight, it was actually kind of funny.

Our tour continued, and although I hoped our team's hard work would overshadow any embarrassing incidents, the awkward moments still lingered in my mind. As a high-performing market, we've accomplished a lot, but I was eager to move past that evening's fiasco. During our travel between facilities, we made a pit stop at a coffee shop for gas and a bio break. It was a chance to regroup, grab a quick coffee, and stretch our legs.

The company VP generously offered to pay for everyone's coffee. Only three of us took him up on his offer. I decided to treat myself to a caramel macchiato. Little did I know this would become another spotlight moment for me. The clerk took an unusually long time making my coffee—about 15 minutes. Meanwhile, everyone else had ordered simple coffee with cream and sugar and had received their orders promptly.

As I stood there waiting, I could feel the impatience of my team growing. Our VP even came up to me and asked what I had ordered that was taking so long. I felt the pressure mounting as everyone sat in their cars, waiting for my coffee. It was yet another moment of unwanted attention. Fortunately, the rest of the visit went smoothly, and no one mentioned the elevator incident or the coffee delay. The focus remained on our performance and how we continued to drive success in a complex market.

About a year later, I was selected for a high-potential stretch assignment with the regional team. It was an exciting opportunity and a testament to my hard work. Six of us were chosen for this prestigious assignment, with different destinations and objectives. Two colleagues went to Las Vegas for the electronics symposium, two to Puerto Rico to learn about Sam's Club operations there, and three of us headed to New York City's fashion district. Our task was to shadow the clothing buyers and learn how they selected merchandise to sell in the stores. We met with fashion designers and owners to preview and design products for potential sale to customers.

Balancing this stretch assessment with my regular duties was challenging. I still had to run my market and manage day-to-day operations. Trusting my team became crucial. They had to handle the business while I was away, and I made myself available for escalations as needed. Having a high-performing team, the market ran smoothly, and I was only pulled in for sporadic support. This allowed me to fully immerse myself in the week-long stretch assignment.

Our journey started with a brisk walk through the city, navigating the narrow and steep stairways of various buildings. Each stop brought us inside the operations of many renowned designers, places I'd only dreamt of seeing. I kept pinching myself to make sure it was real. It wasn't just about observing; I was encouraged to contribute my opinions on materials, colors, zippers, buttons, and more. My suggestions were considered, making me feel like an integral part of the process.

Mid-morning, one of the designers requested an impromptu meeting with our buyer. We had another appointment lined up with a well-known clothing brand, so the buyer instructed me to proceed without her, promising to join me later. Arriving at the next location, I was greeted by the owner and a team of designers, all ready to start the meeting despite the buyer's absence.

As the meeting progressed, the time came to decide on which items we would purchase for resale in our stores. Anxiety crept in; our buyer was still not present. I felt a knot in my stomach as I realized that the responsibility of making these crucial decisions fell on me. Drawing from the experiences from the week, observing and learning from the buyers, I took a deep breath and made the selections. Each choice was a blend of intuition and the knowledge I had gathered. The tension was immense, but I trusted my instincts.

Finally, the buyer arrived just as we were wrapping up. She quickly assessed the situation and reviewed the selections I had made. To my relief and immense satisfaction, she was pleased with my choices. She signed off on the decisions and thanked me for stepping up in her absence. That moment was a significant confidence booster, knowing I could handle such a high-pressure situation successfully.

Reflecting on the day, I realized how much exposure to a different career path could be incredibly rewarding. The experience expanded my horizons, showing me the complexities and excitement of the retail buying world. I almost considered a career switch, but more importantly, I learned the value of stepping out of my comfort zone.

For leaders, I cannot stress enough the importance of giving your team stretch assignments that push their boundaries and expose them to new career paths. These opportunities not only develop their skills but also build their confidence and adaptability. If you are someone looking for growth, sometimes you have to create your own opportunities. Seek out tasks that challenge you and provide exposure, experience, and a chance to scale your abilities.

As I close this chapter, I want to leave you with a message of encouragement. No matter the obstacles you face, remember that you matter, and your potential is limitless. Embrace opportunities that come your way, and don't be afraid to seek out new challenges. You never know what you can achieve until you step out of your comfort zone. Keep pushing forward, and believe in your ability to succeed.

www.ingramcontent.com/pod-product-compliance
Lightning Source LLC
Chambersburg PA
CBHW071350150726
47997CB00002B/928